Cambridge Elements ≡

Elements in the Problems of God
edited by
Michael L. Peterson
Asbury Theological Seminary

GOD AND VALUE JUDGMENTS

Kevin Kinghorn
Asbury Theological Seminary

CAMBRIDGE
UNIVERSITY PRESS

CAMBRIDGE
UNIVERSITY PRESS

Shaftesbury Road, Cambridge CB2 8EA, United Kingdom

One Liberty Plaza, 20th Floor, New York, NY 10006, USA

477 Williamstown Road, Port Melbourne, VIC 3207, Australia

314–321, 3rd Floor, Plot 3, Splendor Forum, Jasola District Centre, New Delhi – 110025, India

103 Penang Road, #05–06/07, Visioncrest Commercial, Singapore 238467

Cambridge University Press is part of Cambridge University Press & Assessment, a department of the University of Cambridge.

We share the University's mission to contribute to society through the pursuit of education, learning and research at the highest international levels of excellence.

www.cambridge.org
Information on this title: www.cambridge.org/9781009475846

DOI: 10.1017/9781009296137

First published 2023

A catalogue record for this publication is available from the British Library

ISBN 978-1-009-47584-6 Hardback
ISBN 978-1-009-29609-0 Paperback
ISSN 2754-8724 (online)
ISSN 2754-8716 (print)

God and Value Judgments

Elements in the Problems of God

DOI: 10.1017/9781009296137
First published online: December 2023

Kevin Kinghorn
Asbury Theological Seminary

Author for correspondence: Kevin Kinghorn, kevin.kinghorn@
asburyseminary.edu

Abstract: Humans continually make judgments that some things have more value than others. Plausibly, it is largely through our value judgments that God intends to guide us in setting priorities and goals. This Element surveys leading accounts of what value judgments *are* exactly. It then explores the particular values we are apparently sensitive to when making two judgments endemic to human life: about what makes a life *good*, and about who *deserves* a good life. Connections are made between differing analyses of human value judgments and views about God's character and the goals God is prompting us to pursue.

This Element also has a video abstract:
http://www.cambridge.org/God-and-Value-Judgments

Keywords: valuing, intuitions, seemings, goodness, desert

ISBNs: 9781009475846 (HB), 9781009296090 (PB), 9781009296137 (OC)
ISSNs: 2754-8724 (online), 2754-8716 (print)

Contents

1 Could Value Judgments Be Communications from God?

In its broadest sense, a "value judgment" might be said to include any evaluative appraisal, including my opinion that pickled herring is disgusting. Colloquial use of that term tends to be narrower, usually indicating one's regard for certain ideals: the values of loyalty, respect, integrity, and the like. When moral philosophers take a step back and offer an analysis of human value judgments, they often do so as a way of addressing a set of related, theoretical questions about why we see certain things as good. In this Element, I will review some leading proposals as to what kind of mental state a value judgment is (Section 2). I will then look at two kinds of value judgments endemic to human life: judgments about what makes for a good life (Section 3) and judgments about why others do or do not deserve a good life (Section 4).

Throughout these discussions, I will note various connection points to theism, in particular to Christian theism. One's analysis of value judgments – what they consist in, how they are formed – has significant implications for the theological claims one can and cannot with consistency go on to make. Conversely, one's theological affirmations may at times lead one to favor one analysis of value judgments over another. A "problem" may therefore arise when one's reflections on one's own value judgments conflict with some favored theological position. Methodological questions can emerge as to whether and when our value judgments *should* take precedence over other sources of theology. But undoubtedly the value judgments we form are *a* source of theology. On the assumption that God created humans with the capacity to make these value judgments, we can plausibly suppose that God's intent is that our judgments will help us identify and prompt us to pursue good outcomes that God intends for our world.

The orthodox Christian position (established at the Second Council of Orange in the year 529) is that any human insight into and attraction to that which is good will originate in God. But is it plausible to think of our value judgments as in fact *revelations* from God, a kind of *communication* from him? In this first section, I will look at the conditions that must be met in order for a value judgment to rightly be called a form of communication from God.

1.1 Forms of Revelation

The main monotheistic religions all claim that God provides us with revelations, or self-disclosures, about his character and plans for our world. These revelations may be general (accessible to all people at all times) or specific (directed to particular persons at particular times). The orderliness of natural laws would be an example of the former, while the incarnation of Jesus Christ would be an example of the latter. In an instance of specific revelation, God's communication to us may be public or private. The incarnation of Jesus Christ now fits in the former category, with an example of the latter being John's vision of Christ recorded in the Book of Revelation.

If we ask *what* it is that God would communicate, one formal answer is that God communicates a message, or a claim that something is so (see Swinburne 2007). This message might come in the form of a sacred text written by human hands. Such a text may be thought to have been dictated by a divine being (cf. the Islamic view that Muhammad received dictation from the angel Gabriel in writing down the Quran). Alternatively, this text might be thought to be in the first instance human discourse (perhaps inspired by God), which is then appropriated by God as God's message to us readers (see Wolterstorff 1995).

Aside from sacred texts, God could in principle appropriate anyone's speech act, offering it as his own speech act to us. We ourselves appropriate others' speech acts all the time in everyday life. For example, suppose you and I attend a training seminar at work. The speaker warns the group gathered of the "dangers of glass ceilings in the workplace." I nudge your elbow and say to you, "Hear, hear!" Through my actions I am appropriating the speaker's message. That message becomes *my* message to you. Further, our unique history together makes it possible for me to communicate an additional message to you: perhaps a message of commiseration that you were passed over for a recent promotion that we both agree you deserved.

How might God appropriate human messages as his own messages to us? In the context of a sacred text like the Christian Bible, Nicholas Wolterstorff's explanation seems most plausible. His view is that it was the canonization of certain texts by the early Christian Church, acting as God's representative on earth and under the direction of the Holy Spirit (1995: 54). Whether and to what extent God inspired the original authors in the writing of these texts would be a separate question. On the present question of what *makes* these texts God's "Word" to readers today, the answer would again be the Church (acting as God's ambassador) declaring them to be God's message to all people.

Aside from public, sacred texts, God could appropriate everyday human discourse as a way of communicating to an individual. Augustine begins the story of his own conversion by recalling a time he heard a child's voice from a neighboring house repeating the phrase, "Take up and read; take up and read." Augustine interpreted this chanting "to be no other than a command from God to open the [Bible], and read the first chapter I should find" (2015: bk 8, 109). One straightforward way in which God could use human discourse to communicate messages to us would be for God to cause us to form the belief that the human message we are hearing is also a message from God to us.

This method of causing us to form certain beliefs would also allow God to communicate more directly to us. Such direct communication might involve hearing an inner, "still, small voice" (e.g., Elijah hearing God's voice in 1 Kings 19). Or it might involve a dream that includes a vision of God speaking to us (e.g., Jacob's vision of God speaking in Genesis 28). On such an occasion I may use inferential reasoning in concluding that God has caused my experience and that God intends me to recognize that he has caused this experience. Less reflectively, I may simply find myself with the belief that God is speaking to me through a dream or through a voice in my head.

I might also form a belief that God is communicating to me while I am listening to a parable or reading a story about a moral exemplar. Indeed, St. Paul made the sweeping claim that God reveals facts about himself to humans through the entire created order: "What can be known about God is plain to them, because God has shown it to them. Ever since the creation of the world his eternal power and divine nature, invisible though they are, have been understood and seen through the things he has made" (Romans 1: 19–20). Drawing from St. Paul's comments and from affirmations in Christian scripture that God has "written his law" on human hearts, the Christian natural law tradition has emphasized our moral awareness as a key aspect of God's general revelation to humans (see Budziszewki 2011).

1.2 Communication As Requiring No Recognition of the Source

Actual communication implies that one has been successful in one's attempt to convey information. Yet, it is possible – and arguably very commonplace – that God may cause a person to form a particular belief, even while the person does not *recognize* that their new belief is a result of divine activity. This point has been key for those theologians who have spoken of the possibility that non-believers might yet have "implicit faith" in God. John Wesley, for example, optimistically spoke of the possibility that "ancient heathens" may well have lived up to the "light they had," having been "taught by God, by his inward voice, all the essentials of true religion" (Wesley 2022).

Suppose that God intends for someone to form a value judgment and ensures that the person does form that value judgment. If the person is unaware that God has caused them to form this judgment, is it still correct to say that they have received *communication* from God?

On one standard definition of communication as "the transmission or exchange of information" (*Oxford English Dictionary*), the answer is yes. An awareness of a communicator's causal role in our belief formation – even an awareness that the communicator exists – is not a prerequisite for receiving communication from them. Consider the practice of subliminal advertising, which can influence our responses to products and our subsequent beliefs about their benefits. I might be subjected to a subliminal message about some food product, Brand X. While later walking through the grocery aisle, it might simply seem to me that Brand X is likely to be more fresh or tasty than its competitors on the shelf. It seems right to say that the advertiser has communicated a message to me, even as I am reflectively unaware of the communicator's role in my subsequent judgment about the merits of the product.

Turning to value judgments, suppose it seems to me on some occasion that some action is good or valuable or ought to be performed. We might suppose that my judgment is the result of a divine intervention in which the Holy Spirit directly caused me to form the judgment. Or we might suppose that there is a long story from evolutionary biology to tell of how God ensured that I would end up forming this value judgment. Either way, if this judgment is caused by God and intended as a form of communication from him, it is not necessary that I recognize these facts or recognize even that God possibly exists. As long as the content of my judgment has in some way been transmitted by God, then my judgment could rightly be called be a communication from God.

1.3 Divine Direction through Noncognitive Avenues

The content of a divine communication may not always be easily expressed in propositional form. This point is in keeping with broader discussions in epistemology. Personal knowledge of someone is arguably something other than knowing a list of facts *about* that person. And the experiential knowledge of *how to* ride a bicycle is surely not reducible to knowledge of a set of propositions. It would be unsurprising if God's communication to us sometimes resulted in types of knowledge beyond a knowledge of facts.

Nevertheless, if God communicates to us in the form of a value judgment, does this communication inevitably involve propositional knowledge: the knowledge *that* something is good or has value? This question is trickier than it might initially appear. Our immediate answer might be, "Yes, surely it's obvious that to *judge* something to be valuable is to *believe* that it is valuable." Yet we will see in Section 2 that some accounts of value judgments construe them as emotional responses. So it is worth asking at this point whether such "noncognitive" accounts of value judgments would automatically rule out these judgments as a form of divine communication.

The Christian scriptures repeatedly allude to the need for God to influence our affective states (e.g., desires, emotions). The Psalmist cries out, "Create in me a clean heart, O God" (Psalm 51:10). And Jesus declared that "No one can come to me unless drawn by the Father who sent me" (John 6:44). The Christian consensus has been that, because of our sinful inclinations, God must enable us to respond to him. What does this "enabling" consist in? On David Hume's model of human action, we are motivated by our affective states and not by our beliefs. Per this model, God's enabling must involve his alteration of our desires or emotions. Choices in line with God's will for us then become psychologically possible as we are attracted to certain ends God intends for us to pursue.

Suppose that God does in some instance cause a person to have a desire that enables them to perform some action. Is it right to say that they have received communication from God? The answer would certainly be yes *if* we further suppose that the person rightly believes that this desire of theirs was in fact instigated by God as a way of directing them to perform this action. God could directly cause them to have this belief, or God could know that they would naturally form this belief when they reflect on their newly formed desire. Either way, when God performs the act of fueling their desires, his goals include the goal of conveying information to them. Specifically, God wanted the person to recognize that their new desire is prompting them toward goals that God intends for them to pursue. God wanted to convey this information, and the information was indeed transmitted.

But suppose that a person does *not* have any awareness that God has in fact fueled their desires as a way of directing them to act a certain way. Could God's act of sparking their desires be said to be a form of communication? As a preliminary point, it may be that God is not actually attempting any communication but is rather trying to elicit a change in behavior. In such a case, we could still talk about the person *responding* to God. After all, in responding to their desires, they are responding to God's prompting. But could God's act of sparking their desires also accomplish a divine goal of communicating to them?

An answer here depends on what exactly we suppose God is attempting to communicate. Clearly God's sparking of their desires is not *itself* sufficient for them to form a belief like "God has sparked in me these desires as a way of directing me toward certain actions." But God's intended message may be more modest than this. Perhaps God merely intends that the person come to believe something like "I ought to perform this action" or "I have an obligation to help this person." If a person's newly formed desires *do* themselves lead them to form such beliefs, and if this was what God intended to communicate through the fueling of their desires, then clearly God *has* transmitted information to them. This point opens the door to the possibility that God might communicate messages to us through our value judgments, even if value judgments turn out to be affective states and not beliefs.

Let me recap some of the main points of this first section. On an orthodox Christian understanding of the role of the Holy Spirit, the beliefs (or desires) we form that move us toward God will ultimately stem from divine activity of some kind. There are a variety of ways in which God could transmit information to us, whether or not we recognize God's role in the formation of our new beliefs. Further, even if we suppose that some message God communicates has propositional content, it is possible that God might communicate this message by influencing our affective states.

Theists are therefore not obliged to hold any one particular account of value judgments: what they consist in and how they are formed. The theist's affirmation that God communicates to us through our value judgments will be compatible with a variety of such accounts. I review and assess some of the leading accounts of value judgments in the next section.

2 Judgments and the Role of Intuition

On the surface, a "value judgment" appears to involve a combination of two quite different mental states. Making a *judgment* is synonymous with reaching a conclusion or forming a belief. But in making a *valuation*, one is taking up a positive or negative attitude toward something, which seems to involve one's desires or emotions.

A helpful way of seeing the difference between cognitive states (e.g., beliefs) and affective states (e.g., desires) is that they have different "directions of fit" with the world. (See Humberstone 1992 for an overview of the history of this term.) Roughly, when my desire for the world to be a certain way conflicts with how the world actually is, there has been no *mistake*. Rather, I will feel impelled to change the world so that it aligns with my desire. Hence, if I want there to be a cup of coffee on my desk, and there is no cup of coffee there, then I will feel some pull to go to the coffee maker and alter the world so that there *is* a cup of coffee on my desk. Desires are said to have "world-to-mind" fit: the world ought to conform to what is in my mind.

By contrast, beliefs have "mind-to-world" fit: they are mental states that ought to conform to what is in the world. When they do not conform, there *has* been a mistake. We might think of beliefs as our "maps" of the world. They are representational in character. As Mark Platts puts it, "falsity is a decisive failing in a belief, and false beliefs should be discarded" so that they "fit with the world" (1979: 257).

Here now is the key question. Do value judgments have mind-to-world fit or world-to-mind fit? That is, are they cognitive states or affective states? Or perhaps a combination of the two? Or possibly sometimes one and sometimes the other? The discussion here is often framed as a debate between *cognitivists* and *sentimentalists*. One difficulty in adjudicating this debate is that each camp can offer a list of initially persuasive talking points.

2.1 The Case for Cognitivism

Cognitivists can begin by pointing to the common language we use in expressing our value judgments. We say things like "I *believe* it is good to honor one's agreements." Others may respond by saying, "I *think* the same thing." While semantics does not settle the nature of moral judgments, it does suggest that we all commonly assume that moral judgments are synonymous with beliefs and have cognitive content.

Second, we use our value judgments as *premises* in reaching further conclusions, just as we do with any other beliefs we hold. I might say, "Since it is good to honor one's agreements, then Sally ought to follow through on her promise to Jim." To deny this point is to face the so-called Frege–Geach Problem. In a nutshell, the problem is that moral terms play the same semantic role in linguistic construction that run-of-the-mill descriptive terms do. (See Schroeder 2008 for a discussion of this objection to noncognitivism, including its genesis in the writings of Peter Geach and John Searle.) Clearly, conclusions like the one about Sally do not follow from *desires*. They again follow from beliefs that serve as premises.

Conversely, and as a third point, we sometimes reason our way *to* a value judgment. I might say, "Since broken agreements cause harm to others, and since harm is bad, then it would be bad to break one's agreements." Here my value judgment about the badness of breaking agreements has been reached through inferential reasoning from premises. But premises only lead me to my conclusion if we suppose that my conclusion is a belief that has mind-to-world fit and therefore ought to follow from true premises. (By contrast, desires don't follow from premises.)

Fourth, the widespread practice of moral disagreement shows the indispensable place shared cognitivist assumptions hold in everyday life. We dispute questions of value with one another. We argue over whether some military campaign – for example, the firebombing of Tokyo during World War II – can be defended as having overall positive value. We argue about whether one good thing (e.g., offering forgiveness to a petty criminal) has greater or lesser value than another good thing (e.g., holding the petty criminal accountable). When doing so, we assume that there is some correct answer that we, but not our opponents, are affirming. If in some instance I am unsure what the correct answer is, I engage in deliberation, trying to arrive at the correct answer. I might sometimes come to change my judgment about the value of some situation, in which case I will believe that I had previously made an *incorrect* judgment. These kinds of disagreements and deliberations obviously would be nonsensical on the supposition that our value judgments were sentiments with world-to-mind direction of fit. We may regret having had a previous desire or emotion, but we hardly think that we or others can be *mistaken* in having a desire or emotion.

Fifth, our value judgments do not always motivate us. This fact undermines the sentimentalist's claim that value judgments simply *are* desires or other affective states with mind-to-world fit. Consider Michael Stocker's example of a jaded politician.

> In his youth, he cared a lot about the suffering of people in all parts of the world and devoted himself to making their lives better. But now he concerns himself only with the lives and fortunes of his close family and friends. He remembers his past, and he knows that there is still a lot he could do to help others. But he no longer has any desire so to do. (1979: 741).

The stipulations of this example seem plausible enough. Surely it is possible to believe that I ought to perform some action, that there is value in doing so – but nevertheless experience no motivation to do it. As further support for this possibility, psychological studies on psychopaths seem to indicate that they can genuinely acknowledge that some action (e.g., of manipulation or cruelty) is wrong or bad. Such an acknowledgment, or belief, seems clearly to constitute a value judgment. Yet psychopaths will lack any motivation to avoid the action in question. They can perform acts of manipulation or cruelty without compunction. So there seem to be clear cases in which our value judgments are formed separately from any sentiment with mind-to-world fit. Once again we are led to conclude that value judgments must be cognitive states with world-to-mind fit.

2.2 The Case for Sentimentalism

Although the case for a cognitivist account of value judgments does seem initially quite forceful, sentimentalists have their own talking points. Taken together, they give us strong reason to reconsider whether value judgments might be affective states after all.

First, sentimentalists will insist that any discussion of value judgments must take into account David Hume's critical point that sentiments, not beliefs, motivate us. Beliefs do *guide* our actions: they explain why we attempt to achieve a desired goal by performing *this* action instead of *that* action. But beliefs themselves are motivationally inert. By contrast, it is the pro-attitudes we associate with desires that move us, impel us, motivate us to act.

Consider now that our value judgments cannot be separated from motivation. To value something is necessarily to have a pro-attitude of some kind toward it. Suppose that someone claimed to value almsgiving but also claimed to have no motivation to help the poor and to have no stronger pro-attitude toward the poor being helped than toward the poor not being helped. Surely we would be right in this case to insist that the person did not in fact value almsgiving! Thus, we will necessarily have pro-attitudes – that is, mental states with world-to-mind fit – toward the things we value.

Now, some cognitivists have claimed that Hume was simply wrong and that some beliefs can themselves motivate (see, e.g., Nagel 1970; McDowell 1979; McNaughton 1988; Dancy 1993; Scanlon 1998; Shafer-Landau 2003; Wedgwood 2007). Yet Hume's point about motivation remains compelling. Desires, by definition, are what provide the felt motivation to perform a given action. And since value judgments are always accompanied by the motivation to change the world if it conflicts with what we value, then value judgments are most straightforwardly explained *as* desires or other affective states.

Second, Stocker's example of the jaded politician was supposed to undercut this necessary link between value judgments and motivation. But examples like the jaded politician are hardly decisive against the sentimentalist position. We are told that the politician judges that there is value in helping others but has no motivation to do so. Yet a point of unclarity arises here that also arises in examples of psychopaths who lack any motivation to avoid certain actions even while, it is claimed, they acknowledge that there is negative value attached to those actions. What is unclear is that the individuals in these kinds of cases are making genuine value judgments. Perhaps by acknowledging the "value" of some actions they are indicating their acknowledgment of what *others* in society deem valuable. Or perhaps they are acknowledging that reasons exist for performing some action, even while these reasons are not *their own* reasons. At any rate, whatever the best description is for Stocker-type examples, we should keep in mind that these kinds of cases are outliers. They are not among the clearer kinds of cases we regard as prototypical in illustrating what is distinctive about making a value judgment. Whatever difficulty the sentimentalist may face in accounting for Stocker-type examples, the cognitivist faces the much greater challenge of explaining why motivation accompanies nearly all (if not all) of our value judgments.

Third, while it is again unclear whether the cognitivist can provide (peripheral) examples of genuine value judgments accompanied by no motivation, what *is* clear is that there are plenty of examples of value judgments that lack cognitive content. These examples come from small children. A small child may witness a loud and violent argument that disturbs her. She may feel a strong aversion to what she sees, and it seems correct to say that her emotional reaction involves a desire or some such world-to-mind affective attitude that these actions not be done. It seems clear that she is viewing the current relational interchanges around her as less good, as having less value, than those inter-changes marked by harmony and laughter. It is true that she will not have fully developed *concepts* like "less valuable" or "harmony," let alone a knowledge of the linguistic terms that correspond to those concepts. Yet her mental and physical responses to the argument clearly align with the responses we associate with a value judgment.

Cognitivism would have us view the child as incapable of making a value judgment, since she lacks an understanding of the concepts (let alone the terms) needed to describe or give cognitive content to her judgment. But this conclu-sion just seems obviously false. Young children are clearly capable of making value judgments on a range of moral and aesthetic matters.

Fourth, a cognitivist account of value judgments lacks the resources to explain the phenomenon of "moral dumbfounding." Participants in psycho-logical studies can judge some action as having negative value, perhaps even judge it to be categorically wrong or taboo. When pressed to defend their reasons for making this judgment, participants may eventually concede that none of their previously expressed reasons actually withstand scrutiny. Yet their value judgments are often recalcitrant. Participants just do not relinquish them, despite now acknowledging that they can think of no good supporting reasons for them.

The obvious conclusion from these cases of moral dumbfounding is that the participants' judgments had not actually been reached by drawing reasoned inferences. Rather, as psychologist Jonathan Haidt puts it, "moral reasoning is generally a post hoc construction intended to justify automatic moral intuitions" (2001: 823). The operative psychological prin-ciple is one of "affective primacy." Our emotional responses and other affective states are linked to the formation of our judgments, with reasoning typically used to justify these responses to others and/or to ourselves. Cognitivist philosophers like to tell a story of how we rational creatures reach beliefs about value by drawing inferences from other beliefs we hold. But social scientists, who conduct empirical studies on actual people, tell a much different story.

Fifth, and as further support for the conclusions just reached from moral dumbfounding, social psychologists have shown that people's value judgments are impacted by a variety of factors that have nothing to do with reasoned inferences. For example, when people are placed in dirty rooms, or otherwise are exposed to disgusting sights or sounds, they subsequently tend to react more harshly when assessing others' moral offences (Schnall et al. 2008; Chapman and Anderson 2013). More generally, situational changes (e.g., ambient sounds, smells, and room lighting) can significantly impact people's normative judgments (Doris 2002; Alfano 2012; Vargas 2013).

Are most of us swept up in widespread irrationality? Surely it is better to say that value judgments, at their core, are affective responses. They are world-to-mind mental states that need neither to be explained nor justified by a process of reasoning. Michael Gill and Shaun Nichols offer this summation: "The empirical work suggests that if we were to restrict ourselves only to ultimate moral principles that could be derived from reason alone, we would be saddled with normative consequences virtually no one is willing to accept." Thus, some version of the sentimentalist position will have to be accepted if we are to hold on to any "commonsense morality" (2008: 155).

Sixth, these experiments by social scientists are reinforced by studies in neuroimaging that point to emotions as uniquely indispensable in our ability to form judgments about value and other normative matters. Changes within those regions of the brain linked to emotions correspond strongly to changes in one's moral attitudes (Greene et al. 2001; Valdesolo and DeSteno 2006; Young and Koenigs 2007). One can continue to make value judgments even when a wide variety of cognitive functions are compromised through brain damage. Yet brain damage that specifically affects the processing of emotional signaling (while largely sparing cognitive functions) has profound effects on moral decision-making (Anderson et al. 1999; Bechara 2004; Koenigs et al. 2007). (See Greene and Haidt 2002 for a brief overview of the trends in psychological studies and brain imaging that led to the enormous amount of literature over the past thirty years linking emotions to moral judgments.)

2.3 The Dual Avenues to Value Judgments

How should we adjudicate the respective cases made by cognitivists and by sentimentalists about the nature of value judgments? An initial puzzlement is that each camp does make certain claims that cannot reasonably be denied. It would be implausible to deny the cognitivist's claim that we do sometimes reach value judgments from inferential reasoning. And our disagreements on matters of value do indicate our widespread assumption that value judgments have descriptive content that is either true or false. At the same time, the sentimentalist offers such a more straightforward explanation why motivation is always, or at least nearly always, connected with value judgments. Further, the findings of social psychologists cannot be ignored: changes to people's value judgments do seem to track more with changes to their affective states than with changes to the supporting intellectual reasons they recognize.

Are we at a standstill at this point, unable to adjudicate the competing, respective cases for cognitivism and for sentimentalism? Happily, we remove much of the puzzlement from our review of cognitivism and sentimentalism when we recognize that there are two broad ways in which we can form value judgments. The respective, compelling points made by cognitivists and by sentimentalists can each be affirmed in at least some cases. We just need to keep in mind that any individual point may only apply to *one* of the two avenues to forming value judgments.

The first avenue involves inferential reasoning from premises. If not formal reasoning, this process at least involves some reflective consideration of what does or does not follow from some piece(s) of evidence. All kinds of evidence may be relevant: reflection on one's own experiences, consideration of others' testimony, and so on. The key point is that one's value judgment is a conclusion reached through a process that involved some deliberation. Descriptive premises lead one to a descriptive conclusion, which of course can then be used in one's further deliberations. When others come to a different conclusion, one will obviously view them as *incorrect* in their belief.

Also important here is that one's reasoned conclusion about value is not necessarily connected to motivation. I might conclude, for example, that some piece of modern art has special aesthetic value and would contribute to the well-being of most people who take the time to study it. I might reach this conclusion because I believe the testimony of art critics who tell me these things and whom I believe to be authorities on these matters. And yet the piece of modern art in question may continue to leave me cold. If cognitivists were right in claiming that jaded politicians and psychopaths can form genuine value judgments, then their judgments will have been reached in this kind of reasoned way. They will be able to appreciate evidence that favors some conclusion about an outcome having value, even while themselves having no pro-attitude toward that outcome.

In sum, key points from the cognitivist can be affirmed: about the place of value judgments in deliberations, about disagreement over value judgments, about outlier cases existing in which value judgments are not connected to motivation. But these points again are applicable *if* we suppose that a particular value judgment has been reached through a process of reasoned inference.

The cognitivist position may not fare so well when we turn to the second broad way in which value judgments are reached. Sometimes we form value judgments in an *immediate* way, with no process of reasoned inference. Such judgments are a matter of *intuition*. It *just seems* to me that some things are good or valuable – in much the way that it seems to me that the wall in front of me is white or that I went to the cinema yesterday.

If these intuitive judgments about value turn out to be noncognitive, affective states, then the sentimentalist's talking points suddenly become very insightful. (Just as the cognitivist's talking points lose much of their force.) Intuitive judgments, as affective states, would naturally involve motivation. Moral dumbfounding would be understandable because these judgments are not necessarily sensitive to evidence. And we would expect that changes to one's emotions caused by ambient sounds and smells would translate to changes in one's intuitive judgments. All this is so *if* it turns out that our intuitively formed value judgments are actually affective states. Are they?

2.4 Intuitive Judgments As "Seemings"

In everyday language, we often say that some action "seems good to me" or that some outcome "seems better than the alternative." Intuitive judgments are indeed a kind of *seeming*. Although intuitive judgments, like perceptions, are formed in an immediate way and not on the basis of evidence, it is better to describe intuitive judgments as akin to a *perceptual experience*. For to call them perceptions may imply that they are *factive*. And a seeming is non-factive – for the same reason it is not a belief. (Timothy Williamson [2000] defines factive attitudes as follows: "A propositional attitude is factive if and only if necessarily, one has it only to truths" [34].)

We can demonstrate these points about seemings by considering two well-known illusions: Müller–Lyer lines and an Adelson shadow figure (see Figures 1 and 2).

Looking at the Müller–Lyer lines, the horizontal line on top seems plainly longer than the one on the bottom. But we get out a ruler to check the lines, and we see that the lines are actually of equal length. We now *believe* that the lines are equal, and there is no serious temptation moving forward to waver in this belief. Nevertheless, when we have another look, the appearance of the lines

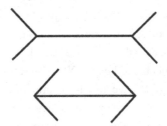

Figure 1 Müller-Lyer lines

Figure 2 Adelson shadow figure

remains compelling: it still *seems* that the line on top is longer. (See Peter Railton [2014] on how intuitive judgments are "compelling" in that they can persist "in the face of contrary conscious judgment" [815].)

Corresponding points apply to the Adelson shadow figure. At first glance, it seems obvious that the A-square is darker than the B-square. This appearance may seem so compelling that we seriously doubt that they really are the same shade of gray. So we diligently cut up an index card in order to meticulously cover everything in the picture except those two individual squares. We now see clearly – and now firmly believe – that the squares really are the same shade of gray. We take away the paper tidbits and have another look at the whole picture. The appearance is still absolutely compelling, and we wonder how something that seems so clear could yet mislead us.

Intuitive value judgments can likewise come apart from our beliefs about the matter. A committed utilitarian may respond to Philippa Foot's famous trolley example by restating their belief that it is overall a good and right thing to intentionally cause one person's death in order to save five others. But the idea of actually pushing a large man onto train tracks – which we suppose is the only way to divert the train and save the five – may still seem bad, objectionable, abhorrent to this committed utilitarian. As other examples, drill sergeants and disciplinarian parents may have to steel themselves in order to carry through with actions they believe are warranted and justified, even as it may seem to them in the moment that their own actions are harsh or even cruel.

These kinds of example do, I think, serve as knockdown arguments against the view that intuitive judgments are beliefs. Yet the "seeming" constitutive of an intuitive judgment *does* still have mind-to-world direction of fit. When the Müller–Lyer lines seem to me to be the same length, it is not that I *want* them to be the same length. Rather the lines present themselves to me as an apparent feature of the world. Further, this seeming *disposes* me to form an accompanying belief (i.e., the belief that the lines are the same length). And I will go on to form this belief if the belief is not defeated by considerations of counterevidence (e.g., measuring the lines with a ruler). In this way, we might speak of a seeming "attracting" a subsequent belief.

In short, intuitive value judgments, as seemings, are non-inferential, non-factive, and they attract belief. Should we say that a seeming *itself* qualifies as a "judgment"? Or is it better to say that a resulting *belief* from the seeming would constitute the judgment? I do not think a lot hinges on this question, which can be settled by stipulation. The important question remains: what kind of mental state is a "seeming" about value? I will continue to use the term "intuitive judgment" to denote this kind of seeming. But I would not quibble with someone who wants to distinguish a "seeming about value" from the "intuitively reached judgment (i.e., belief)" to which the seeming gave rise.

Thus far I've said that an intuitive value judgment is a kind of seeming. We might list various kinds of seemings in a taxonomy: perceptual seemings (e.g., the Adelson squares seeming to be different shades) and intellectual seemings (e.g., seeming to remember buying milk yesterday). Value judgments belong to a particular class of seemings that are broadly about *normative* matters: what there is value in doing, what it is good to do, what one ought to do. These seemings share an important, unique feature. They have mind-to-world direction of fit *and* world-to-mind direction of fit. Like any other seeming, the world presents itself to us in a certain way. Uniquely, though, when it seems to me that some object or outcome is valuable (or ought to be achieved), then I necessarily have a pro-attitude toward it. Sentimentalists were right to emphasize this point. It really would be nonsensical for me to say, "It seems to me that thing A has more value than thing B, but I in no way prefer A to B."

If we seek to explain the dual directions of fit of an intuitive value judgment, we have two options. First, we could maintain that such a judgment, or seeming, is a cognitive state of some kind (even if not a bona fide belief). The challenge then becomes explaining why this particular cognitive state is also motivating (i.e., also has world-to-mind direction of fit). Alternatively, we could maintain that an intuitive judgment is an affective state. That takes care of the motivational element. But the challenge then comes in explaining the mind-to-world fit of a seeming about value.

I regard the first option as a hopeless enterprise. On cognitivist accounts of intuitive value judgments, there just is no way to account for the *inherent* motivation within the seeming itself. Mike Huemer, who views all intuitions as "intellectual appearances," makes the only move I can see as available to the cognitivist. He remarks that a moral intuition is "an intuition whose content is an evaluative proposition" (2005: 102). But this move will not do. As Antti

Kauppinen points out, "purely cognitive states (states with only a mind-to-world direction of fit) cannot move us to act, whatever their content" (2013: 367). At least this is so on the Humean model of motivation. (For a wide-ranging and convincing defense of Hume's model, see Sinhababu [2017]).

Does the second option fare better? I think it does. Intuitive value judgments can be seen as a kind of *emotion*, formed in particular contexts. Emotions, as affective states, can obviously provide the motivation associated with intuitive value judgments. And because emotions can be *directed to* various objects (or actions or states of affairs), we can explain the mind-to-world fit that an intuitive value judgment also has. While this second option holds promise, it does require us to consider carefully the nature of an emotion. And it requires us to see why intuitive value judgments in the end are best classified as "quasi-perceptual" experiences.

2.5 Emotions and Thick Judgments

Intuitive value judgments once again have dual directions of fit. Our task in this section is to identify the kind of psychic state constitutive of an intuitive value judgment. We must not think of this task as one of identifying some mental experience comprised of both cognitive and affective *states*. Rather, the task is to identify a single *psychic state* comprised of both cognitive and affective *elements*. Linda Zagzebski explains, "To my ears the term 'state' already suggests separability, whereas 'aspects' clearly does not" (2003: 109). When intuitive value judgments are made, it is not that a person comes to be in some cognitive or perceptual state *and then* forms an affective response to that prior state. Such cognitive and affective states would not necessarily be connected, and they indeed come apart in cases like Stocker's jaded politician. Rather, an intuitive value judgment is a single, *thick* judgment, to use Bernard Williams's term.

Williams famously introduced "thick ethical concepts" (Williams 1985). These concepts contain both descriptive and evaluative aspects. Examples include "contemptible," "pitiful," "rude," "courageous," and "treacherous." For these concepts, it is not as though we *add* an evaluative component to a mere description. Rather, the evaluative and the descriptive are necessarily intertwined in the very concept itself.

Zagzebski rightly points out that thick evaluative judgments are "ground level" judgments in that we all begin to make them early in life. ("That was mean." "That was unfair.") These judgments can admittedly be "thinned" as we reason through their implications and engage in discourse about them. We may at some point become emotionally detached from our original judgments as our judgments now shift toward serving more theoretical purposes (Zagzebski 2003). Hence we may at times appreciate the fact *that* a person is pitiful or treacherous without instinctively reacting to the person *as* pitiful or treacherous. But the original point still holds: a thick evaluative judgment is a single psychic state necessarily comprised of both cognitive and affective aspects, or elements. What is crucial for our purposes is of course that value judgments reached intuitively, or immediately, are thick in this way.

I suggested earlier that an *emotion* is a good candidate for being this "thick" psychic state that contains dual directions of fit. It is uncontentious that emotions are "intrinsically motivating" (Alfano et al. 2018: §3.3). Might they also have the kind of representational component characteristic of mind-to-world fit? One historically prominent (though flawed) view of emotions would quite clearly allow for a representational component. Paul Thagard and Tracy Finn observe that "Since the Greek stoics, many theorists have argued for the view that emotions are cognitive appraisals concerning the extent to which something aids or hinders our goals" (2011: 151). Thus, my emotion of happiness when seeing the sun shining is caused by, or perhaps we should say it *is*, my assessment that the sunshine is conducive to my goal of enjoying a picnic in the park.

There are severe problems with the cognitive appraisal account of emotions (sometimes called "judgmentalism"). It does seem to guarantee mind-to-world fit. Oddly, it does so at the expense of guaranteeing world-to-mind fit (which is one of the uncontentious hallmarks of an emotion). A cognitive appraisal is after all synonymous with a *belief.* And beliefs once again are not intrinsically motivating. Further, infants clearly do have emotions, even as they are not yet capable of making contentful appraisals. Last, a cognitive appraisal account of emotions is unable to explain why emotions can be recalcitrant in the face of our all-things-considered appraisals. Suppose that I am visiting the Grand Canyon and approach a viewing deck extending over the cliff's edge. I may look at the glass floor of this viewing deck and believe that it is structurally sound and that it will certainly hold my weight. But with my long-standing fear of heights I still experience a fair amount of disquiet when I step out onto it! So there seem to be some telling objections against the view that emotions are cognitive appraisals of some kind.

Thagard and Finn note that "Since the nineteenth century, the major alternative to the cognitive appraisal theory of emotions has been the somatic perception theory, according to which emotions are perceptions of bodily states" (2011: 151). Somatic theories emphasize the differing feelings that correspond to changes in bodily states: raised heartbeat, adrenaline, and so forth. In his own well-known somatic account of emotions, Jesse Prinz argues that, if our brains are wired to interpret certain bodily changes as representing, for example, danger, then we can indeed come to fear a bear because we perceive it as dangerous. But we perceive this dangerous quality of the bear indirectly, by means of perceiving our bodily changes (Prinz 2007).

Somatic accounts of emotions (sometimes called James–Lange accounts – see James 1884 and Lange 1885) offer important insights into the connection between emotions and bodily states. But they are also surely flawed.

On somatic accounts, my bodily sensations indicate indirectly to me that some object has some feature (e.g., that a bear is dangerous). But it is much more credible to view our emotional experiences as direct responses to objects or situations themselves, even as these targets of our emotions also cause bodily sensations. Uriah Kriegel remarks, "As an adolescent, I experienced grief at my grandfather's death; somewhat trivially, the grief was intentionally directed at my grandfather and his death, not at inner bodily changes (if such there were) consequent upon the realization and emotional processing of his death" (2015: 133). The generalized problem is that somatic accounts offer an implausible explanation of the intentional content of an emotion. Emotions (typically) do have a target. They are directed *to* something. But they are directed to objects and environments and imagined scenarios, not (primarily) to bodily states.

We are still exploring the possibility that intuitive value judgments might be emotional responses. To evaluate this suggestion, we need a correct account of what emotional responses are exactly. We have seen that both of the more traditional accounts of emotions have problems. Happily, an alternative account of emotions has emerged in recent years. It seems to be the most plausible way of understanding emotional responses in general. It also allows us to see how an emotional response actually has all the characteristics of an intuitive value judgment.

2.6 Intuitive Judgments As Quasi-Perceptions

In light of the difficulties with cognitive and somatic accounts of emotions, so-called perceptual accounts of emotions have gained traction among a number of philosophers and psychologists in recent years. A good example is Robert C. Roberts's description of emotions as "concern-based construals." Construals are "impressions, ways things appear to the subject" (2003: 75). So the representational, mind-to-world aspect of an emotion is clearly preserved, and Roberts is happy to talk of emotions as "a kind of perception" (87). At the same time, since our "concerns" arise out of our existing network of desires, the world-to-mind aspect we associate with emotions is also preserved.

Of course it is one thing to *state* that an emotion is a kind of perception that also happens to have an evaluative aspect. But we need to say more in order to *show* that some kinds of perceptions are indeed connected to concerns or other evaluative attitudes. After all, many kinds of perceptions do not necessarily involve any evaluative component. When I perceive a bird on a ledge, I may or may not value the scene before me. Even when the nature scene does seem valuable to me, this mind-to-world evaluation is still extrinsic to my perception itself. If we are to think of an emotion *as a kind of perception*, is there a helpful way to think about the necessary connection between perception and evaluation?

Anthony Kenny offers a useful beginning point by distinguishing *particular* objects from *formal* objects of emotions (Kenny 1963). Andrea Scarantino and Ronald de Sousa explain, "Any *X* that I can have emotion *E about* is a particular object of *E*, whereas the formal object of *E* is the property which I implicitly ascribe to *X* by virtue of having E *about X*" (2021: §4). Thus, when I stumble upon an angry bear while camping, the bear would be the particular object, or target, of my emotion of fear. But the formal object would be something like: "that which endangers me."

So is it that we *perceive* a feature like "dangerousness"? This is the suggestion of Christine Tappolet, who describes emotions as "perceptual experiences of evaluative features, such as fearsomeness or admirableness" (2018: 495). But Kauppinen raises the question of what story most plausibly explains our perception that something is, for example, dangerous or admirable or wrong. He asks, "Is the wrongness of an action the sort of thing that can cause us to have a feeling of disapprobation?" Surely it is more plausible to think that what we perceive are properties of the particular (as opposed to the formal) object of an emotion – "such as the shooting of a peaceful demonstrator by a police officer" – which we then "respond to . . . with an emotional reaction, which construes the action as wrong" (2018: §5.1). Returning to the example of the bear, I don't observe the bear's "dangerousness." Rather, I observe the *bear*, which of course I do construe as dangerous.

If it is not quite right to say that we are "perceiving evaluative features" when we form emotional responses constitutive of intuitive value judgments, then what is the best way of understanding the connection between perception and evaluation? One key is to recognize the sense in which an emotional response might be called a "quasi-perception." When I "see a bear," I see it through faculties of visual perception. When I, in addition to this visual perception, "see a bear as dangerous," the bear does *seem*, or *appear*, dangerous to me. Yet it is my *affective* states (with mind-to-world fit) that produce this seeming, or appearance. As Peter Goldie remarks, "Emotional feeling toward an object (typically toward the object of the emotion) is a feeling towards that thing as being a particular way or as having certain properties or features" (2000: 58). That is, the emotional response of "seeing the bear as dangerous" is a manifestation of my sentiments (or my "concerns," to use Roberts's language).

We are still exploring the view of emotions that understands them as a kind of perception. Our key conclusion thus far is that my emotional response of "seeing a bear as dangerous" is itself a manifestation of my sentiments. But does this undermine our working assumption that emotions are a kind of perception (with mind-to-world fit)? Recall that we cannot account for an emotion's dual directions of fit by claiming that I have a visual perception and then (contingently) also have a desire to be far away from the bear. That would be two psychic states. Rather, the perceptual experience is itself supposed to be a "thick" one in that it necessarily contains both affective and cognitive elements. I've said plenty to reinforce the affective element of an emotion. What about the cognitive element? If emotions are manifestations of sentiments, can they have a mind-to-world aspect?

The answer is yes. I have said that the best model for understanding emotional responses is to view them as a kind of perception. Admittedly, there is an obvious difference between an emotional response and a visual perception (like seeing a bird on a ledge). An emotional response is "thick" in that it has dual directions of fit. Given its affective feature, it is probably best to call an emotional response a *quasi-perception*. Still, an emotional response remains perception-like. Importantly, the features it shares with most other perceptual experiences are enough to establish its necessary, mind-to-world aspect.

We can say this because of the central role that *phenomenology* plays in how we understand perceptual experiences in general and the justification they give for subsequent beliefs. (Phenomenology refers to the way an experience feels to us.) Suppose I look out on the ledge and immediately form the belief that a bird is resting there. If someone asks me to defend the rationality of my belief, I could only respond by saying that, well, it sure *seemed* to me that there was a bird resting there. And indeed we all assume that this "feel" of a perceptual experience makes it rational for me to proceed on the assumption that things probably are as they seemed to me. Without this shared assumption, we wouldn't be rational in trusting *any* of our perceptual experiences.

Emotional responses, as manifestations of sentiments, will have a certain phenomenology: a phenomenology that represents the world as being a certain way. This last point is borne out by the growing research over the past twenty years on "phenomenal intentionality," which Kriegel defines as "the intentionality a mental state exhibits purely in virtue of its phenomenal character"

(2013: 2). Early in this research program, Terence Horgan and John Tienson argued that phenomenal mental states have "intentional content that is inseparable from their phenomenal character" (2002: 524). Thus, as Kauppinen observes, "Part of what it is like to have an experience of a red object . . . is to experience the colour as belonging to an external, persisting object distinct from one's flow of experience itself. The experience is directed outwards, as it were, in virtue of its phenomenal character, which suffices to endow it with conditions of accuracy" (2013: 370).

We are of course ultimately interested in how things might appear to us to have certain evaluative properties. Kauppinen again offers a helpful example, asking us to consider a case in which we view someone as blameworthy for some action: "It is not as if we have some brute, directionless bad feeling or sensation combined with either belief or intuition that the target did something wrong. It is rather a part of what it is like to have the feeling that its target appears to call for a negative response" (2013: 371). So when we examine the phenomenal character of an emotional episode, we find that the target (e.g., a person who has stolen) of the emotion appears to us to have certain properties (e.g., blameworthiness). And this point holds even on the supposition that our emotional responses are manifestations of our sentiments.

Here's the key takeaway point. The phenomenal qualities of an emotional response are adequate to provide the mind-to-world representational aspect of an intuitive value judgment. To have an emotional response *is* to have the world seem to us to be a certain way (a bear *as* dangerous; a child's smiling face *as* precious). Still, keep in mind that an intuitive value judgment is not a belief (even while it attracts belief). Like any other immediately formed "seeming," an intuitive value judgment can be recalcitrant in the face of one's own contrary belief. (Recall the way it may seem to a committed utilitarian that sacrificing one person to save five is offensive.)

We are finally at a place where we can sum up our discussions on the makeup of intuitive value judgments. Intuitive value judgments are best viewed as emotional responses, with these emotional responses being manifestations of sentiments. As mental attitudes with world-to-mind fit, motivation is naturally intrinsic to these emotional responses. At the same time, an emotional response is directed *to* an object (or event or state of affairs). And the phenomenology of this response is such that the object *appears* to have positive or negative value. With objects appearing, or seeming, to be a certain way, the emotional response constitutive of an intuitive value judgment has much in common with other kinds of *perceptions*. But because this response is actually a manifestation of sentiments, the response is best categorized as a quasi-perception.

2.7 Implications for Spiritual Formation

We turn now to what is at stake theologically in these discussions. The fields of moral philosophy and moral psychology have offered insight into the nature of value judgments: how they are formed and what they consist in. These insights have significant implications for how theists can – and perhaps should – understand the process of spiritual formation. Theists will of course be interested in epistemic questions of how we hear from God. From Section 1, our value judgments are one critical way in which God may communicate to humans. Thus, theists will naturally be interested in questions of how we can *better* hear from God through the value judgments we make and, relatedly, what may *keep us* from forming value judgments that reliably are communications from God.

Christian theists have widely supposed that one acquires greater knowledge of God and God's will for us largely through a method of *catechesis* (literally, "instruction"). One learns the biblical narrative of God's interactions with humankind. One learns the core doctrines of the Church and often the more specific emphases of a particular denomination. Suppose I am a student presented with religious instruction about the ends that God values for our world and invites us to pursue with him. Why might I believe that the claims I hear are true? John Locke offered one answer.

> God when he makes the prophet does not unmake the man. He leaves all his faculties in the natural state, to enable him to judge of his inspirations, whether they be of divine original or no … If he would have us assent to the truth of any proposition, he either evidences that truth by the usual methods of natural reason, or else makes it known to be a truth which he would have us assent to by his authority, and convinces us that it is from him, by some marks which reason cannot be mistaken in. Reason must be our last judge and guide in every thing. (1975: bk. 4, ch. 19, §14, 704)

So we might use reason to assess the *content* of a purported revelation or, more modestly, to determine *whether* a purported revelation really is from God. (Locke had in mind the latter role for reason.) But inferential reasoning of some kind remains the basis for the beliefs God leads us to form.

All this is not to say that, on Locke's approach, the Holy Spirit must be sidelined from any role in our inferential reasoning. The Christian theist may emphasize that God must move us, direct us, draw us if we are to form beliefs – including value judgments – that are forms of communication from him. But the role of the Holy Spirit here will be one of enabling us to see the good reasons that do exist in support of the Church's claims about God and the valued ends God seeks for us to pursue with him. Christian theists have often described the state of fallen humans as marked by "spiritual blindness" (see Kinghorn 2005: ch. 6). The key to overcoming this blindness would then be God removing the obstacles that keep us from using inferential reasoning in reaching conclusions about such matters as the valuable ends we should pursue.

One potential problem with this general approach to catechesis is that it runs counter to the way in which people usually form value judgments. Recall the two ways in which value judgments can be formed: (1) through inferential reasoning, and (2) through immediately formed "seemings." A proliferation of psychological studies over the past thirty years strongly suggests that this second way of forming value judgments is far more prevalent than the first way.

Pyschologist Daniel Kahneman coined the phrase "fast and slow thinking" to describe the two ways we reach conclusions (Kahneman 2011). The first pathway is fast, intuitive, and heavily linked to emotional responses. The second is slower and deliberate, making use of inferential reasoning. Fellow psychologist Jonathan Haidt uses the metaphor of a "rider and an elephant" to depict the respective roles that deliberate reasoning and emotional responses play in forming normative judgments (Haidt 2012). Reason can indeed direct our thought processes, just as a calm elephant can be directed by a human rider. An agitated elephant is of course a different matter. Once our emotions become engaged, reason will have little power to influence the direction of one's thoughts and conclusions. Reason comes to play the role of a "rational tail" wagging behind an "emotional dog," to use another of Haidt's metaphors (Haidt 2001). One's use of reason is not so much to reach normative conclusions but rather to *justify* the more immediate, emotionally based conclusions one has already reached.

The distinction between fast, emotionally based processing and slow, deliberative processing may not be as neat and tidy as some of these models suggest (see Evans 2012; Kahane 2012; Cushman 2013). Nevertheless, the psychological studies over the past few decades do offer strong evidence that our normative judgments are more typically a product of our emotions than our deliberative reasoning. And, as mentioned previously, this conclusion is reinforced by studies in neuroimaging showing that the regions in our brain linked to emotions have a unique and indispensable place in our ability to make value judgments.

These findings from psychology and neuroscience have profound implications for how religious catechesis might (and might not) most effectively be approached. At least on the specific matter of helping others make normative judgments – including judgments about value – instruction that invites inferential reasoning may be of limited usefulness. Theists have sometimes debated the *premises* from which one should reach normative conclusions: Should we take our own experiences as reliable evidence for normative truths? Should we accept the Church as an equal authority to the Bible in discerning God's priority of valuable ends? While these debates have significance in their own right, they operate on the shared assumption that people are using inferential reasoning in reaching their conclusions. Yet, if value judgments are more typically the result of emotional responses, then the invitation to reason from premises – of whatever kind – may again be of limited effectiveness.

The Christian tradition has always recognized the broad point that our desires and other affective states do impact our decision-making and beliefs. I noted earlier the more intellectual emphasis on doctrinal affirmations as a core part of catechesis. But the Christian tradition has also emphasized the indispensable roles of *acts of piety* (e.g., prayer, corporate worship, Bible reading, Christian community) and *acts of mercy* (e.g., feeding the hungry, welcoming the stranger, visiting the sick and imprisoned). These acts of spiritual formation are aimed at transforming one's affective attitudes at least as much as one's cognitive states.

Christian theists have sometimes disagreed about what the *core* of our resistance to God is. This disagreement naturally extends to the question of how God most fundamentally needs to help us if we are to be spiritually transformed. One view is that *pride* lies at the root of human sin, with God needing to lead us toward humility if we are to receive the further transforming help that God wants to give us. This broad view can be found in the writings of Augustine and in the Roman Catholic tradition of spiritual formation that includes such figures as Thomas à Kempis and Teresa of Ávilla. By contrast, Martin Luther, John Calvin, and John Wesley saw pride more as a symptom of a deeper spiritual problem: that of unbelief. God must first open our eyes to important truths about him and about the moral laws in his created order. Only then can we make progress in actually following God's laws and being transformed within that journey.

I offer no sweeping conclusions here on the multidimensional topic of spiritual formation. Forming value judgments that more accurately reflect God's judgments is but one aspect of our broader formation. But I do note that the Augustinian tradition focuses on an affective component of human disposition. And the findings of psychological studies are once again that our value judgments are more commonly the result of affective components like emotion than any cognitive component. Hence, if God is to communicate to us by moving us to form value judgments, it is plausible to suggest that he may tend toward leading us to have certain emotions – as opposed to leading us primarily by helping us see certain truths through inferential reasoning.

Accordingly, if the Church aims to help others form those value judgments through which God intends to direct them, it will need to focus on formation practices designed to shape their affections in suitable ways. A robust theology of human emotions may thus prove to be a vital resource for the Church.

2.8 Theological Commitments about How We *Should* Make Value Judgments

In the previous section, I considered how an analysis of the nature of value judgments can inform theistic practices of spiritual formation. We could perhaps describe that discussion as advice from philosophers and psychologists to the theologian about how effective spiritual formation *can* be done. But the theologian may well bring existing concerns about how spiritual formation *should* be done. More specifically, one's theological commitments may lead one to a certain view on the ways in which humans should (and should not) form value judgments. It is all well and good for the philosophers and psychologists to offer insights into how people typically *do* form value judgments. But might there be theological reasons to insist that God intends for us to form value judgments in a particular way – irrespective of how often we do form them in that way?

Thomas Aquinas contended that authentic Christian faith requires one to believe the Christian articles of faith on very particular grounds, namely on the authority of the Church. Even if one's beliefs aligned with the teachings of the Church, the use of natural reason to assess the claims of the Church would indicate a failure to acknowledge the Church's God-given authority. Aquinas, stated that, if a person "holds what he chooses to hold, and rejects what he chooses to reject, he no longer adheres to the teaching of the Church as to an infallible rule, but to his own will." If such a person is not prepared to follow the teaching of the Church in all things, it is evident that person "has not the habit of faith" indicative of one who submits to divine truth. (1947: II–II, 5, 3). Aquinas does defend the project of natural theology in which we use our reason to draw inferences from self-evident truths and from our observations of the natural order. But only *some* beliefs are appropriately reached this way. Those truths knowable by natural reason would not be among the "articles of faith," but would instead be "preambles to the articles; for faith presupposes natural knowledge" (I–II, 2, 2).

Value judgments would arguably fall under Aquinas's list of beliefs permissibly acquired through natural reason. Still, the broader point I am raising is that one may have theological commitments that demand that various religious and moral beliefs – including value judgments – be based on God's authority. That is, the demand would be that a person's belief be the result of one's recognition that God has directed us to accept the proposition in question. Given that this recognition and subsequent belief will involve inferential reasoning, the theist with the kind of commitments we are discussing may thus insist that people's value judgments really should stem from reflection on God's (or the Church's) authority. Accordingly, value judgments really *shouldn't* be reached through immediate, emotional responses.

Aquinas is representative of the view that inferential reasoning has a proper place in determining *whether* a purported revelation really has come from God (even as the content of that revelation may be something we could not have acquired through reason). But a different kind of theological commitment may lead the Christian theist to eschew any use of inferential reasoning in determining whether one's newly formed value judgment might indeed be a divine directive.

Karl Barth is representative of the broad fideist tradition that insists that we must "start with revelation." In his defense of "Reformed theology" over the methodology of "natural theology," Barth emphasized that revelation comes to us as we encounter God directly. This revelation "is a ground which has no higher or deeper ground above or below it but is an absolute ground in itself, and therefore for a man a court from which there can be no possible appeal to a higher court" (2004: 305). When God communicates something to us, the knowledge we gain through this encounter "does not therefore permit the man who knows to withdraw himself from God, so to speak, and to maintain an independent and secure position over against God" (1938: 103). For Barth, when God causes us to form a belief, there simply is not space for us to use inferential reasoning in assessing the likelihood that this new thought of ours really is true. God communicates to us more directly, more compellingly, more immediately.

As a side note, theists in the Reformed epistemology movement of the past few decades have defended the rationality of forming religious beliefs in an immediate, non-inferential way (see Plantinga 2000). They allow that some people perhaps do form beliefs about God through inference. But they claim that, as an empirical matter, it is more typical for God to cause people to form religious beliefs in an immediate, non-inferential manner. Barth, however, had deeper theological reasons for rejecting the possibility of receiving true knowledge from God as a result of our own inferential reasoning.

Consider now the two ways in which we can form value judgments. We can reach them through inferential reasoning or, more typically, they can be the result of an emotional response. Those theists in the tradition of Barth may, contra Aquinas, actually be more theologically comfortable with the idea that

God would spark in us an immediate, emotional response than that God would lead us through a process of inferential reasoning.

Barth's understanding of the Fall contributes to his reluctance to allow a role for inferential reasoning in arriving at beliefs about what God has communicated to us. He understands human sin to have so blinded us to truths about God that a dramatic, direct encounter with God is needed for our minds to be reoriented in a way that allows us to see religious and ethical truths. Christian theists have certainly held differing views on the nature and extent of the Fall. I simply note here that one's theological commitments on this topic may once again have implications for how one thinks we should make value judgments.

Barth's working assumption was that our reasoning processes have been compromised. Joseph Butler's warning was that we would be well advised to do *more* reasoning – and to do it in a "cool hour." He chastised the "Enthusiasts" of his day for allowing the passions to dominate the way they understood God. Passions do have their place, Butler acknowledged. But even the "fear of God" should stem from (i.e., be inferred from) a settled belief that God is perfectly just and perfectly good (2017: s. 13, §2). The general point is that, for those theists who view human sentiments as primarily susceptible to sinful corruption, it may be more natural to think of God helping us form value judgments through the avenue of inferential reasoning than by means of emotional responses.

As God seeks to help us mature spiritually and overcome the negative effects of sin, does God primarily focus on healing and restoring our cognitive faculties or our affections? Different theologians have emphasized different aspects of God's transforming grace. Some have focused on the ways in which God's transformation of us can "cure reason" (Erasmus 1969: 50). Others have discussed God's sanctifying grace more in terms of God's restructuring of our "disordered loves" (Augustine 2009: bk. I, ch. 27, 18).

Still other theologians may have such a strong doctrine of sin and the Fall that they are led to conclude that we will forever in this life be incapable of making value judgments that align with those of God. Consider the stark claim of Luther:

> You may be worried that it is hard to defend the mercy and equity of God in damning the undeserving, that is, ungodly persons, who, being born in ungodliness, can by no means avoid being ungodly, and staying so, and being damned, but are compelled by natural necessity to sin and perish … But inasmuch as He is the one true God, wholly incomprehensible and inaccessible to man's understanding, it is reasonable, indeed inevitable, that His justice also should be incomprehensible; as Paul cries, saying: "Oh the depth of the riches both of the wisdom and knowledge of God! How unsearchable are His judgments, and His ways past finding out" (Rom. 11:33) (2012: 314–15).

Luther here contrasts "our judgment" with "God's judgment." Does he mean that we really will be incapable in this life of making value judgments that align with God's judgments?

An answer here depends on what we suppose is involved in "making judgments." Certainly the avenue of reaching a value judgment through an emotional response is ruled out. Luther is right to think his readers will be worried at the idea of God unilaterally deciding to redeem some humans and damn others, as an expression of God's perfect will. Speaking for myself, such a decision seems decidedly less good than a decision to redeem all humans! But Luther does go on to say that we can *believe* what the scriptures (as Luther interpreted them) affirm about God's unilateral decision to redeem some humans and damn others. We form such a belief "as we are instructed" (2012: 317), even if this affirmation continues to seem counterintuitive to us.

We discussed earlier how value judgments can be reached through inferential reasoning, even as they continue to seem mistaken to us. So there does seem room here for Luther to grant that we can form value judgments that align with God's value judgments – *as long as* our judgments are based on inferential reasoning and as long as the evidence for this reasoning process stems from God's revelation in scripture (and not from our own intuitions or experiences). In short, the Lutheran view does allow that God can communicate to us through our value judgments. But the avenue to reaching these judgments would be very particular, and the judgments themselves may continually be at odds with what seems valuable to us.

Let me offer some summary points of this larger second section on the nature of value judgments. We started by looking at the two different ways in which we can form them. We can form them on the basis of inferential reasoning, in which case motivation will not automatically accompany the judgment. More typically, though, we will form them in a more immediate way. Some outcome or state of affairs will *seem* to us to be valuable. These seemings are most plausibly viewed as directed emotions, with those emotions themselves being quasi-perceptual experiences with dual directions of fit.

While those discussions took some time to flesh out, we have now seen that they have important implications for understanding spiritual formation. Philosophers and psychologists can offer important insights into how value judgments are formed. Theists of course will be interested in how our value judgments can come to be consistently the ones God intends for us to form. (Different theists may of course have different lists of the particular value judgments that God is understood to affirm.) If value judgments are indeed predominantly emotional responses, then directors of spiritual formation would do well to explore the question of which emotions do and do not lead to the kinds of value judgments God intends for people to form. In line with this point, spiritual instruction will need to involve helping others recognize the phenomenology of suitable emotions – and of course helping others cultivate them.

The contributions of philosophers and psychologists may, however, also raise certain *problems* for the theist. Whatever the findings from empirical studies on the ways in which people typically *do* make value judgments, the theist may have various theological commitments that lead them to insist that our value judgments *should* only be cultivated in specified ways. It may be that the theist will agree with Hume in complaining that the great error of Western philosophy has been to overemphasize the role that reason can and should play in guiding our actions and controlling our passions. If so, then the theist may welcome the recent empirical studies on the important links between our value judgments and our affective states.

On the other hand, the theist may have theological commitments that lead them to advise that we mustn't allow our emotions to determine our judgments about value. Instead, we should reach our value judgments through inferential reasoning. Perhaps the theist will insist that our judgments should be inferred from propositions we accept on God's authority. Perhaps the theist will contend that our value judgments should result from reflection on the things to which God assigns worth, as revealed in scripture or as taught by some Church tradition. Perhaps the theist will understand the effects of sin to have so warped our affective states that we can only come to share God's value judgments by reasoning our way to them. (After all, they will continue to *seem* suspect to us in some ways, as long as our affective states are so misaligned.) Perhaps the theist will simply view humans emotion as fickle and thus advise that we would do well to base our value judgments on the more stable foundation of reasoning. In short, the theist for whatever reason may be committed to the view that God's plan is to lead us through reasoning to form value judgments that align with his own. An analysis of value judgments that links them to immediate, emotional responses may therefore just show the extent of the *problem* that must be overcome if our value judgments are to serve reliably as communication from God.

We will see this kind of problem – that is, this potential dissonance between philosophical analysis and theological commitment – reemerge in Sections 3 and 4. In these final two sections I will look at two kinds of broad value judgments we all commonly make. In Section 3, I will look at our judgments about what makes our lives *good* or not. Then in Section 4, I will explore why we think it valuable that people receive the kind of life they *deserve*. Philosophical analysis of these two kinds of value judgments has the potential to provide important insights for the theist on a range of doctrines and affirmations about the character of God. But the theist may also find their previous commitments on these theological matters challenged by a philosophical analysis of goodness and of desert.

3 Judgments about the Good Life

A core affirmation of Christian theism is that God is good. Many Christian churches begin worship services by saying aloud together, "God is good – all the time!" Theologians include goodness among the core attributes of God, along with omnipotence and omniscience (Swinburne 2016). Indeed, Aquinas followed Augustine in explaining that God is the "supreme good" (Aquinas 1947: I, 6, 2; Augustine 1887: bk. I, ch. 2). The methodology of so-called perfect being theology likewise identifies God as "perfectly good" or "maximally great" (Hill 2005; Nagasawa 2017).

In contrast to gnostic traditions, Christian theism affirms that the material world God created is good. In the opening pages of Genesis, we read that "God saw everything that he had made, and indeed, it was very good" (Genesis 1:31). The reader is invited to share this judgment that our world is indeed good (and by extension that God the creator is good).

Christian eschatology affirms that God's activity is leading toward a good end for creation. God through Jesus Christ is redeeming our fallen world. Christ is building his Kingdom. And the culmination of human history will involve the redeemed coming to share in perfected relationships in heaven through which they will attain ultimate joy.

Yet, in affirming that God is good, that God's created world is good, and that certain future outcomes are good, various questions remain. What exactly are theists claiming when they state that "God is good"? In what sense is the created order good? What makes some outcome (or action or state of affairs) good? And finally, on what basis do we judge someone's life to be a good one? The philosophical conclusions we reach in analyzing the nature of goodness may impact how we understand theistic claims that God or that creation is "good." Equally, one may have theological commitments that lead one to insist that certain analyses of *goodness* must be mistaken because they are (perceived to be) at odds with those theological commitments.

3.1 How We Understand the Concept "Good"

If we were to ask about the *property* something has that makes it good, we would be asking about the *nature* of goodness. But there are also questions about the *meaning* of the term "good." What exactly do we mean when we attribute goodness to some person or action? How did humans ever come up with this concept – *good* – in the first place?

Looking at the etymology of the term, Alasdair MacIntyre traces its use to the social, functional role it played in early Greek society. Specifically, "the word ἀγαθός, ancestor of our *good*, is originally a predicate specifically attached to the role of a Homeric nobleman." To be good (ἀγαθός) was to be "kingly, courageous, and clever." To judge a person to be good and *not* kingly, courageous, and clever would not be to make "a morally eccentric form of judgment." Rather, it would be to utter "an unintelligible contradiction" (1998: 4).

The term "good" (ἀγαθός) was always both descriptive and evaluative. But over time, the conceptual link was lost between the term and the *specific* description of a Homeric ideal. Changes to societal roles and expectations naturally led to differing views about which characteristics are ideal or commendable. Accordingly, differing views emerged as to the conditions under which it is appropriate to offer the positive evaluation that something is "good." William D. Ross thus commented that the best way to understand the historic use of the term is to see it as one of "indefinite commendation" (2002: 66).

Ross's account of the etymology of the term "good" seems plausible as far as it goes. We might still ask how a person becomes a competent user of that term. Do we grasp a corresponding concept, *goodness*, which is simply primitive (akin to the way *redness* is primitive in that we cannot analyze it using further concepts)? Or are we able to understand the concept *goodness* because we have an appreciation of further, more primitive concepts?

George E. Moore famously took the first option, insisting that the concept *good* is unanalyzable (1993). Consider the way in which we understand certain objects to be yellow. We see that daffodils and lemons and canaries have a shared property, which we conceptualize and name as "yellow." On the Moorean story, we see (as a matter of moral intuition) that some things have a certain normative property, which we conceptualize and name as "good."

But there is an alternative and, I think, decidedly more plausible story to tell about how humans come to appreciate the meaning of the term "good" (see Kinghorn 2016: ch. 1). On this story, the concept *good* is not primitive. We come to appreciate its meaning only because we have an appreciation of further concepts that *are* primitive. Specifically, we have an appreciation of what it is to flourish (versus not to flourish).

From the earliest age, we humans have a variety of either positive or negative experiences. We experience what it is like to feel hungry and to have full stomachs. We experience what it is like to feel cold and to feel comfortably warm. We experience what it is like to feel isolated and to feel the hug of a loved one. In short, we have experiences of our lives going well for us as we live them, and, conversely, we have experiences of our lives *not* going well.

As sentient creatures capable of reflection, we can appreciate this difference between flourishing and failing to flourish. My point is not that all humans from the earliest age will appreciate the concepts and accompanying terms "flourishing" and "well-being." My point is rather that, when we do form these concepts, they are primitive. We experience our lives *as* going well for us. Our mental experiences contain intrinsic qualities that are pleasurable or unpleasurable, and we do not appreciate this difference by referencing *other* concepts.

It is our appreciation of this difference between flourishing and not flourishing, I suggest, that best accounts for our ability to appreciate the concepts *goodness* and *badness*. We understand the conceptual distinction between *good* and *bad* by referencing our own experiences of flourishing versus failing to flourish. We naturally have a pro-attitude toward our own flourishing – and by extension the flourishing of those we care about and whose interests we have made our own. Hence, describing something as "good" becomes a way of commending it as furthering our or someone else's well-being.

3.2 Semantics and Our Use of the Term "Good"

Various objections might be raised against this claim of a conceptual link between goodness and well-being. One kind of objection involves semantics. We do make statements such as "swimming is good for Sue." But we also make plenty of other statements about what is good – without referencing any subject's well-being. Consider such claims as "That is a good knife"; "She is a good person"; "That drawing is good"; "It is good that people be happy." In these cases, we are either attributing "good" to something (in the first two statements) or predicating "good" of something (in the last two statements). In all the cases, if we take our language at face value, we are not referencing anyone's well-being.

In predicating "good" of some object or state of affairs, we seem to be stating that it is good in and of itself, or that it has *final* value. As a quick side note, I to say that something is good "in and of itself" is to say that it has *intrinsic* value. To say that something has "final value" is to say that it has *noninstrumental* value. Strictly speaking, intrinsic value is not the same as noninstrumental value, as Christine Korsgaard (1983) explains. Still, in the discussions that follow, I will use the terms "intrinsic value" and "noninstrumental value" interchangeably, though I will be primarily interested in noninstrumental, or final, value.

Back to our use of language, which again sometimes suggests that we have judged something to be good aside from any consideration of whether it happens to be instrumentally good *for* someone. Looking at our attributive uses of "good," sometimes our claims are easy to link with well-being. Plausibly, a "good knife" would be one that aids a person in, for example, cutting a steak with ease. But in other cases when we attribute "good" to something, it is harder to see how our attributions might be conceptually linked to our consideration of anyone's well-being. James Griffin remarks that "a good Roman nose is merely one that has the defining characteristics to a high degree." Because these characteristics of a nose serve no "function or role or purpose," there is therefore "no interest being served" (1996: 39–40).

These objections based on semantics, though, are far from decisive. As an initial point, in everyday language, we often use ellipsed talk in predicating something of an object. When I point to a car on the road and say, "That car is old!" I mean that the car is old for one that is still roadworthy. When I comment on a dog being "really large," I mean that the dog is large for a dog (i.e., that it is large as dogs go). Judith Jarvis Thomson points out that we may often say "That is good" as a way of saying "That is good in respect R." But if we don't know which respect is relevant when we hear a speaker describe something as "good," then "we don't know what property the speaker is ascribing to the thing" (2008: 9–10). Thomson here is following Peter Geach, who remarked that "there is no such thing as being just good or bad, there is only being a good or bad so-and-so" (1956: 34).

From this starting point that our descriptions involving "good" will often be ellipsed talk, the door is now opened for a semantic analysis of "good" that might plausibly link it to subjects' well-being. Paul Ziff offers just such an account, insisting that our use of the term "good" is our indication that something "answers to the interests" of some (real or imagined) subject (1960). There may admittedly be *derivative* uses of the term. For example, a farmer may lament that a "good amount of rain" is forecast for tonight, even while his fields are already flooded. (Presumably "good" and "large" became interchangeable because typically a large soaking of rain *is* helpful for vegetation growth and thus for farmers.) But if we can think of no subject's interests that could be at stake, then the use of "good" in a sentence will be unintelligible. Thus, Ziff explains, the phrase "That cadaver is good" makes sense (think of medical researchers), but the phrase "That corpse is good" does not (1960: 215).

Stephen Finlay focuses his semantic analysis of "good" by examining the structure of our sentences (2014). He surveys the varied ways we use the term "good" in our references to subjects and actions and states of affairs. (*S* is good for *X*; *S* is good with *X*; *S* is good at *X*-ing; *S* is good for *X*-ing; and so on.) Finlay concludes that there *is* a unified, logical form to all our uses of the term "good." Specifically, this relation is one of being "good for." Thus Finlay arrives at a conclusion about the meaning of "good" that is very similar to the one from Ziff. We can describe something as "good" only as we can reference some subject's interests. Despite the varied ways we use the term, references to things being "good" ultimately make sense only as references to them being "good for" some subject.

Even if one does not find this semantic analysis conclusive, it nevertheless is plausible enough to undercut the force of the first objection I mentioned to the claim that a conceptual connection exists between goodness and well-being. That first objection was from semantics: specifically, that some of our expressed judgments about goodness clearly lack any reference to anyone's well-being. We have seen that this objection turns out not to be a forceful one. Our descriptions of things as "good" are often ellipsed talk. And plausibly the meaning of "good" is always connected to what is "good for" some subject.

3.3 Goodness Versus Goodness-For

So a semantic analysis of how we express judgments about goodness – for example, "God is good"; "God's creation is good" – will not be decisive. What other kinds of objections might be leveled against the claim that goodness is conceptually linked to well-being? To clarify a point here, no one would claim that our judgments about goodness are *never* linked to anyone's well-being. Clearly, some things are good because they are good *for* someone. We would ordinarily decry cutting another person's abdomen with a knife. But we view such an act as (instrumentally) good when done by a doctor for the purpose of removing a patient's inflamed appendix. The critical question is whether we sometimes judge something to be good *aside* from any consideration of how any subject's interests or well-being is affected. Do we sometimes recognize things as intrinsically good, or good in and of themselves? (Sometimes this question is asked in terms of whether some things have the property of "goodness simpliciter.") If semantic considerations don't settle the issue, how might it be settled?

It is common at this point for the defender of goodness simpliciter to assert that we all just plainly *see* that some things are good in their own right. It is just *obvious* to us that a Rembrandt painting is better, has more intrinsic value, than a painting produced by a beginning art student attempting their first watercolor. As discussed in Section 2, the judgment here does not stem from any reasoned inference. The judgment is immediately formed, a matter of intuition.

The link between goodness and beauty is instructive. Robert Adams notes how the ideas of the Good and the Beautiful often played the same role within Plato's writings. Adams describes the kind of goodness at stake (goodness simpliciter): "It is not *usefulness*, or merely instrumental goodness. It is not *well-being*, or what is good for a person. It is rather the goodness of that which is worthy of love or admiration" (1999: 13). Adams considers "excellence" probably the best synonym for "good" in this context. The kind of goodness in question is "exemplified by the beauty of a sunset, a painting, or a mathematical proof, or by the greatness of a novel, the nobility of an unselfish deed, or the quality of an athletic or a philosophical performance" (83). The crucial point is that, when judging something as "good" in this context, we are *not* responding to a relational property (such as being good for someone). Rather, we are responding to the intrinsic value of the object – a value we again just intuitively *see* as obvious.

Some may not find this intuitive appeal convincing (see Kinghorn 2016: ch. 2). It is after all an entirely contingent matter that we humans should judge a Rembrandt painting or a Mahler symphony as excellent. We can imagine a world in which all the creatures in it evolved to have complex melodies constantly running through their heads. With such a cacophony of sounds running through their heads, only a select few – the musical geniuses – could disentangle the glut of constant, intersecting music patterns everyone experiences in order to write a clear, simple song like "Blue Suede Shoes." Yes, in our own world, the complexities of Mahler's *Resurrection* symphony challenge and inspire us, and Elvis Pressley's simple song is mundane to our ears by comparison. But this again seems an entirely contingent matter. And that point arguably undercuts Adams's intuitive appeal that we are actually responding to the (objective) excellence, or goodness simpliciter, of things we judge to be beautiful, noble, and worthy of being called "good."

Notwithstanding this rejoinder to Adams, many people do find convincing the kind of intuitive appeal he makes to intrinsic goodness (whether aesthetic or moral). Yet we would do well also to consider a very different kind of intuitive appeal that the *welfarist* wants to make. Welfarism is the view that the goodness of anything is ultimately a matter of its being *good for* someone. The well-being of subjects is the only final, or noninstrumental, value. Borrowing Thomas Nagel's language, I will understand a subject as capable of a well-being if there is something "that it is like to *be* that organism – something it is like *for* that organism (1974: 436). This requirement of sentience allows subjects to experience their lives *as* going well or not well for them.

Here now is the intuitive appeal the welfarist will offer. Imagine two possible worlds. Now consider that someone has suggested that one of these worlds is *better* than the other. Wayne Sumner describes the welfarist's intuitive response:

> If something will improve the conditions of no one's life, make no one better off, then what ethical reason could be given for recommending it? And conversely if something will harm no one, make no one worse off, what reason could be given for condemning it? (1996: 192).

So suppose someone suggests to me that our current world has taken a turn for the worse. Yet this person cannot name a single subject who has experienced her life as going any worse for her. Indeed, no one's life *has* been made any worse. Whatever changes have been made to the world, they have in no way affected anyone's joy, peace of mind, or any other aspect of anyone's well-being. The changes to the world have not even *potentially* affected anyone's well-being – that is, they have not made it any more likely that anyone's well-being will be negatively affected at a later date. In such cases, I would be at a complete loss to understand why I should think the world has taken a turn for the worse. This at least is the welfarist's intuition about the nature of goodness.

So we arrive at two competing appeals to intuitive judgments, represented by Adams and by Sumner. If a beautiful Rembrandt painting is destroyed by fire, this event would certainly be bad for people in the future in that they would miss out on the benefits of viewing it. But would this event *also* be bad just because something of intrinsic value – something of excellence, or goodness simpliciter – has been destroyed? Sumner admits that his kind of thought experiment does not amount to a "proof" against the existence of "non-welfarist basic good." But he thinks the non-welfarist has the burden of proof in any stalemate. The welfarist can at least plausibly explain why we value such things as beauty, knowledge, and achievement: we see them as good for us and for others. And "since foundational values should not be multiplied beyond necessity," the burden of proof is on the non-welfarist to show why a property like goodness simpliciter is needed to explain our judgments that various things are good (1996: 203). Adams of course will insist that our judgment that some things are "worthy of admiration" just *is* an awareness of the intrinsic goodness of these things. So we really do have competing appeals to intuition here as to what our judgments about goodness amount to.

I'll note a final kind of objection to there being a conceptual link between goodness and well-being. Against the welfarist position, some have claimed that our judgment that something is "good for" someone actually *presupposes* a prior judgment that this something is good in its own right. Stephen Darwall labels as "the Aristotelian Thesis" the view that "the good life consists of excellent (meritorious or worthy) activity." Darwall himself maintains that the truly good life for humans will be one in which we engage in activities "through which we come into appreciative rapport with agent-neutral values, such as aesthetic beauty, knowledge and understanding, and the worth of living beings" (2002: 75). In like manner, Joseph Raz maintains that "in justifying that anything is good for any agent we show (*a*) that the thing is good, and (*b*) that the agent has the ability and the opportunity to have that good." In this way, "relational goods presuppose non-relational ones" (1999: 260).

Yet any sweeping claim that welfarist judgments presuppose judgments about goodness simpliciter does not hold up to closer scrutiny. Christian Piller considers a case in which a motorist has to turn left in order to avoid hitting a pedestrian. It is certainly good for the pedestrian that the motorist turn left. But clearly it does not make sense to say that the motorist's "turning to the left" is an intrinsic good and that the pedestrian "has it" (2014: 199–200). So welfarism cannot be rebutted on the grounds that our judgments about welfarist value necessarily presuppose our prior judgments about non-welfarist value.

What has emerged from our discussions are two very different ways of understanding our judgments that some things are "good." Accordingly, two different views emerge as to how God might seek to guide us through our judgments about goodness. Does God intend for us to see the intrinsic goodness of certain things? Or does God intend only for us to recognize the way in which some things are good for subjects? In Section 3.4, I will look at how God might want us to form the judgment that "God is good." In Section 3.5, I will look at the judgment that "God's creation is good." Finally, in Section 3.6, I will look at our judgments about what a "good life" consists in.

3.4 God As (the) Good

Adams understands the goodness of things to lie in their *resemblance* to God, who alone is the "infinite good." His view has clear affinities with Plato's view that the things of our world are good insofar as they participate in the *form* of goodness. Augustine provided an early integration of Platonic themes with Christian theism, maintaining that we should not love the things of this world (even other people) for their own sakes. Rather, we should love them solely "for God's sake" (i.e., because they participate in God, who alone is both the "supreme good" and the source of all goodness) (2009: bk. I, ch. 27, 18).

Christian theists writing downstream of Plato have not merely contended that God exemplifies the property goodness (simpliciter). The claim has also often been that "God *is* the Good." David Baggett and Jerry Walls comment that this view "has a venerable history within Christianity. Thomists, Anselmians, theistic Platonists, and theistic activists, including such contemporary analytic philosophers as Alvin Plantinga and Adams, all concur that on a Christian understanding of reality, God and the ultimate Good are ontologically inseparable" (2011: 92).

Given Plato's own particular theory of Forms, it is certainly understandable that he would be committed to an ontology of Goodness not reducible to what is good *for* subjects. But of course few people today would want to uncritically adopt Plato's theory of Forms. So it is reasonable for us to ask if there are elements of his metaphysical framework that we would want to retain and that offer support for the claim that we perceive God's goodness (simpliciter) when we judge that "God is good." As it happens, actual argument is not typically offered for this claim. Rather, an appeal is typically made to immediate, intuitive perception. As Baggett and Walls remark, "We are inclined to think that the ultimate ontological inseparableness of God and the Good is something of an axiomatic Anselmian intuition; a vision apprehended, not just the deliverance of a discursive argument" (2011: 93).

A theist who embraces welfarism will perhaps be more committed to the idea that we *do* use inferential reasoning in forming the judgment that "God is good." We come to believe that God, as creator, is the source of life. And we come to believe that God is benevolent – that is, he is committed to the ultimate flourishing of us creatures he created. As one who is both committed to our flourishing and able to bring it about, we commend God as "good." Put another way, we come to recognize that God is good for us and for others.

In short, one's philosophical commitments to the nature of goodness can impact how one understands the theological claim that "God is good." If one understands *goodness* to be an irreducible, non-relational property that we apprehend intuitively, then in judging God to be good we are appreciating God's excellence, or his intrinsic property of goodness simpliciter. On the other hand, if one understands *goodness* as relational – a matter of what is good *for* some subject – then in judging God to be good we are reflectively appreciating the way that God is *life* itself and imbues with life all those who are rightly related to him. So one's philosophical commitments can indeed impact one's view about what exactly we are responding to (i.e., what aspects of God's nature) when we form the judgment that "God is good."

Conversely, one may have existing theological commitments about the nature of God that, one believes, require certain philosophical conclusions about the nature of goodness. Oliver O'Donovan insists that various biblical passages clearly identify God with goodness itself. He points to Psalm 119:68 as particularly clear: "Good art thou, and doest good." So, yes, God does indeed *do* things that are good for us. But O'Donovan emphasizes that there is the prior point that "he *is* the good that he *does*." That is, God is the good that "stands behind" other goods. As the *source* of goodness, God can then provide good things to us. Hence, O'Donovan remarks, we find Christian scholastic philosophers speaking of the "*bonum diffusivum sui*, or self-imparting good": In God's acts, we meet the one who *is* goodness and who does good (O'Donovan 2021).

John Cottingham similarly emphasizes God as the source of goodness. He objects to the idea that the theist could start with the idea that certain things are good for us – and then simply add "the extra metaphysical claim that the world was divinely created" (2011: 57). The suggested problem with this kind of welfarist framework is that "good-making properties" would exist in our world "whether or not the world was created by God" (55). God would no longer be the *source* of goodness, as depicted in the biblical picture of God and creation.

Questions do seem to remain about what exactly does and does not follow from this theological emphasis on God as the source of goodness. O'Donovan is correct that certain biblical passages do seem to identify God with goodness. Yet one might also ask about the methodology of using the particular phrases of biblical authors (particularly in poetic passages like the Psalms) to settle philosophical questions about the ontology of goodness. As to the claim that God is the "source" of goodness, the Christian welfarist will agree that God is the source of life and that only in being rightly related to God can we attain a life of highest flourishing. The Christian welfarist might then press the question whether any orthodox doctrinal commitments would actually be lost if we denied that God has some intrinsic property, goodness simpliciter. Still, the broader point remains that, for theists who *do* have theological commitments that, they believe, require God to have this intrinsic property, they will have reason to reject any philosophical arguments that goodness is reducible to what is good *for* subjects.

3.5 The Goodness of Creation

The Hebraic and Christian scriptures, in contrast to Plato and later gnostic traditions, depict God's physical creation as good. Instructive here are the repeated, divine judgments God is described as making in the creation accounts of Genesis 1–2. At every stage of creation, we find the refrain: "And God saw that it was good." The reader is of course invited to share this judgment about the goodness of God's creation. But what good-making properties are we supposed to see?

One answer is that we are to see the final value of creation itself. We see it as (objectively) beautiful. We see it as excellent, or as having the property of goodness simpliciter. This is not to say that we consciously identify this property, goodness simpliciter. But the point is that we are called to have a positive evaluation of creation, in addition to and distinct from any instrumental sense in which we view creation as being good for us.

A different answer will be given by those who are persuaded by welfarist arguments about the nature of goodness. God's creation will be seen as good inasmuch as creation is good for us and for other creatures with a well-being. Admittedly, some of God's pronouncements of the goodness of creation in Genesis occur before the introduction of sentient creatures. Yet we can still read these pronouncements as declarations of the prospective ways in which the physical creation is good for any subjects who inhabit it. Thus, the value of the sun, the rain, the rhythm of day and night, and so on will have instrumental value in that these parts of creation contribute to the well-being of biological life-forms capable of having lives that can go better or worse for them.

In support of this reading of Genesis, we can note that the Hebrew word for "create" (*bārā'*) plausibly refers to "creating functions" over against "physical creation" (see Walton 2009: ch. 3). Thus, the description of God's creative acts in Genesis 1 would be a description of the functions God intends the various, physical parts of our world to play. And these functions, the welfarist will emphasize, are foremost to bring forth abundant life for living things, especially humans who are to steward the rest of the created order as God's image-bearers.

In short, there is no single, "face value" reading of the references to goodness in Genesis that would point us to one particular view of the nature of the goodness of God's creation. The Hebrew word *tôv,* translated as "good" in the Genesis passages, has very wide connotations and can indicate moral goodness or beauty or usefulness. One dictionary of biblical Hebrew states that *tôv* "means 'good' in the broadest sense possible. It includes the beautiful, the attractive, the useful, the profitable, the desirable, the morally right" (Richards 1995: 315–16). Another dictionary of biblical words notes that the uses of the word "good" throughout the Bible "are clearly prephilosophical in content." They "generally reflect ordinary uses of the term" and "do not seek to clarify 'the good' in distinction from other moral categories, such as 'right' or 'appropriate,' or to develop some kind of value theory or alternative philosophical hypothesis" (Green 2011: 332).

One could of course *begin* with a philosophical commitment to the property goodness simpliciter and then conclude that God's pronouncement over creation must be an allusion to this property. But I do not see how God's pronouncement offers any special support for this view over the welfarist's account of goodness as a matter of what is good *for* subjects.

If *tôv* in Genesis *is* interpreted as "intrinsic goodness," then the welfarist's understanding of goodness becomes problematic. But again *tôv* can just as plausibly be interpreted as indicating the *usefulness* of the created order. On that interpretation, the goodness of creation lies in the way it achieves the ends for which God created it. Specifically, these ends will chiefly involve the ways in which the created order affords us humans opportunities to attain abundant life.

3.6 The Good Life

To speak about the ends God intends for us is to raise the issue of in what a "good human life" consists. Assuming that God intends for us to attain our long-term highest flourishing, leading a good life will at least partly consist in leading a life that is good *for* us. But on Christian theism, is there more to a good life than a life that is good for subjects?

The Westminster Shorter Catechism famously declared that "the chief end of man is to glorify God, and to enjoy him forever." Let us suppose that this is an accurate description of a good human life. Is there *one* end to be pursued here? The Christian welfarist might say yes, claiming that our enjoyment of God *is* what glorifies God. Other Christian theists have denied that there is anything like a necessary connection between the two. Indeed, some have claimed that God is glorified by the sufferings of the reprobate in hell (see, e.g., Tertullian, *De Spectaculis*: ch. 30; Peter Lombard, *Sentences*: bk. 4, dist. 50; Aquinas 1947: suppl. III, q. 94; Edwards 1835). Typically the claim is that God is glorified because his justice is displayed – along with his unmerited favor on the redeemed, which they are able to appreciate more fully as they witness the plight of the reprobate.

Christian non-welfarists will acknowledge that enjoyment of God is *one* way in which God is glorified. But the key point is that there are *other* ways in which God is glorified. And really, so the claim will go, it should be obvious that a life that glorifies God will not always be a life that is good *for* the one who lives it. Think of the early Christian martyrs!

In response, the Christian welfarist can accommodate the point that our *short-term* well-being will not always coincide with a life that glorifies God. Suffering clearly does have its place in the Christian life. But the Christian welfarist will view any pains associated with Christian virtue only to be *instrumentally* valuable. They make possible a life of ultimate, eternal flourishing that itself has final value. The attainment of *this* final value is what glorifies God.

The assumption behind the Christian welfarist's claim is that God's single, ultimate goal for us is that we fully enjoy life with God and with other creatures who also participate in a community of perfected relationships. All other goals God has for us are subsumed under this single, broad goal. God may at times act mercifully toward us or may act to discipline us or to preserve just outcomes. Yet all these commitments are subsumed under the broad commitment God has for us to attain our highest flourishing. When we *do* move toward this end for which God created us, then God is glorified. Hence, for the Christian welfarist "enjoying God" and "glorifying God" amount to the same thing. They equally describe "the good life." This welfarist position does commit one to a particular understanding of what we might call God's moral attributes. Benevolent love becomes *the* central divine attribute. All other moral attributes will be derivative of that central attribute.

Other Christian theists will hold a different view of God's nature. God's love, justice, and holiness might be seen as *incommensurable*. Adopting this

theological framework, God's commitment to justice or to holiness will sometimes come at the (final) expense of people's well-being. God can be glorified
when *these* aspects of his character are displayed. Given that a good life is one
that glorifies God, it follows that a life could be a good one by glorifying God –
even if this life does not (ultimately) go well for the one who lives it.

Earlier we noted Adams's view that finite things are good insofar as they
resemble God, who is infinite goodness. The Christian welfarist may allow that
a good life for us will, as it happens, always resemble God's life in some way.
But for the welfarist, this resemblance is not what *makes* a life a good one. What
makes it a (noninstrumentally) good life is that it goes well for the one who lives
it. And since from the Christian welfarist perspective this is the one, overriding
goal God had in creating us, then when our lives go well for us God is glorified.

All this is not to say that, on the Christian welfarist position I have been
outlining, our own flourishing will be the *goal* we ourselves seek to achieve.
Welfarism is not the same as (either psychological or ethical) *egoism*. It may very
well be God's intention that *we* should flourish only as we prioritize the flourishing of *others*. (Cf. Jesus's statement: "Those who want to save their life will lose
it, and those who lose their life for my sake will find it" [Matthew 16: 25].) This
picture of flourishing through self-giving, interdependent relationships is very
much a Trinitarian picture of the flourishing life of Father, Son, and Holy Spirit.

The idea of flourishing only as we intentionally seek the flourishing of others
raises a final question. Can we contribute to *God's* flourishing? That is, can we
properly seek as a goal God's well-being? Some Christian theists have rejected
that idea. Thomas Weinandy remarks that the classical Christian tradition views
God as one who "does not undergo successive and fluctuating emotional states;
nor can the created order alter him in such a way so as to cause him to suffer any
modification or loss" (2000: 111). Thus it would be a mistake to think that we
might impact God's life as God experiences it. Yet Weinandy also acknowledges
a sea change among Christian theologians from the end of the nineteenth century.
As a result, he observes, many (if not most) theologians today do affirm that our
actions can impact God's experiential life. I myself side with this latter group. If
we can "grieve the Holy Spirit" (Ephesians 4:30), and if God joins in the
"rejoicing in heaven over one sinner who repents" (Luke 15:7), then it is difficult
not to think that our actions can impact God's well-being in some ways. If this is
right, then the welfarist judgment about what makes for a "good life" – and how
we can contribute to others' lives being good ones – will extend to God's life.

To summarize the discussions of Section 3, we looked at our judgments that
things can be *good*. We asked how we humans came to understand the meaning
of that term. And we explored the kind of corresponding property, *goodness*, we
are "seeing" when we see that something is good. What emerged from these

discussions are two broad ways of understanding human judgments about goodness. On one view, we recognize that certain things and activities are *intrinsically* good. They have a kind of excellence to them: something about them that makes them worthy of admiration, if one only has eyes to see it. On the alternative (welfarist) view, we appreciate the ways that certain things and activities are good *for* subjects capable of a well-being. Stemming from our own experiences of flourishing, we naturally view the well-being of ourselves and those we care about as having final, or noninstrumental, value. Other things may instrumentally contribute to well-being, and we thus view those things as having instrumental value.

As we have seen, this broad debate about the nature of goodness – *goodness simpliciter* versus *goodness-for* – has implications for various theistic claims. One's philosophical commitments here will impact how one understands our judgments that "God is good," that "God's creation is good," and that God endeavors for us to lead a "good life." Equally, one's theological commitments on these matters may require one to endorse a particular philosophical view about the nature of goodness. So philosophical commitments may both inform and also present problems for one's theological conclusions, and vice versa.

4 Judgments about Who Deserves a Good Life

In the previous section, I looked at our judgments as to what makes for a good life. In this last section, I will examine our judgments that some people, but not others, should enjoy a good life. That is, I will explore why we think there is value in people getting what they *deserve*.

4.1 The Importance We Place on Getting What One Deserves

Fred Feldman brought out the point that we all think of pleasurable experiences as being "intrinsically good," or having positive value. But he also emphasized that this positive evaluation we naturally give to positive experiences is "adjusted" when we consider whether the person having the positive experiences is *deserving* of them. Thus, when a virtuous person has a pleasant experience, this "positive desert enhances the intrinsic goodness" of this pleasure. On the other hand, when a vicious person has the same pleasant experience, the person's "negative desert mitigates the intrinsic goodness of the pleasure" (1995: 575–6). The same kinds of enhancement and mitigation are operative with *painful* experiences. Yes, they are intrinsically bad. But they are less bad when they happen to vicious people and more bad when they happen to virtuous people.

Can the positive, intrinsic value we place on pleasure ever be *overridden* by considerations of whether the person deserved that pleasure? Feldman notes that some moral philosophers have indeed contended that it can be an overall *bad* thing for a vicious person to experience pleasure and, correspondingly, an overall *good* thing for such a person to experience pain. Moore was one such philosopher. He offered examples such as cruelty in which any enjoyment one gets from the action would be "evil in itself" (1993: ch. VI, §§124–5, 256–7). Moore was part of what Thomas Hurka calls "a golden age for moral theory," the period in British moral philosophy from Henry Sidgwick to Ross that included Hastings Rashdall, Harold A. Prichard, Charlie D. Broad, and Alfred C. Ewing. Hurka observes that, during this time of rich moral theorizing, "two commonly accepted objective values were virtue and desert," with desert understood, as Ross put it, as "the proportionment of happiness to virtue" (Hurka 2001: 6; Ross 2002: 27). Immanuel Kant anticipated these kinds of value judgments in stating that the highest good is happiness "in exact proportion with the morality of the rational beings who are thereby rendered worthy of it" (1899: 456).

These philosophers are merely giving voice to what we all surely feel intuitively. I will volunteer that as a child, I woke up with my brothers on Saturday mornings to watch the weekly black-and-white Western shown on TV. We would patiently endure fifty-five minutes of watching outlaws steal from, intimidate, and otherwise run roughshod over the honest, well-meaning cattle ranchers and shopkeepers of a local town. We would endure this tense viewing in order to delight in the final five minutes of the show when the sheriff finally gives the outlaws their comeuppance. Without that final chapter in which the vicious outlaws are held accountable, the storyline would have been a moral outrage for us children.

Movies, novels, and plays of all kinds inevitably have virtuous and vicious characters. Revenge-themed dramas like *The Count of Monte Cristo* are the most obvious types of stories in which we want to see retribution exacted on the vicious characters. But other types of stories are not much different. In a detective story, we want to see Sherlock Holmes triumph *and* we want to see Moriarity defeated. In a romantic tale, we want to see characters like Darcy and Elizabeth finally married *and* we want to see those who meddled in their romance reproved. Our approval of a villain's downfall is not merely a case of *schadenfreude*. As Kristján Kristjánsson explains, that feeling is linked to "malicious envy." By contrast, when we see a vicious person meet with a bad outcome, what we experience is "satisfied indignation" as our "sense of justice" is restored (2006: 96–100).

Just how much importance do we place on people getting what they deserve? Listening to everyday conversations, it seemingly is *the* issue that trumps all others in terms of whether moral redress is needed. If we became convinced that everyone in the world had received exactly what they deserved, seemingly we would be concluding that no one has actual grounds for complaint. We might still work to *address* people's situations and, in charity and love, work to make their lives better. But there would not be the felt need for redress, that kind of unsettled feeling we might describe as perceived "moral imbalance" in the world. This felt need for redress leads us to say such things as: "Arsenal may have won the match on a poor referee's decision, but Liverpool deserved to win that day"; "Steve may be the oldest child, but he hardly deserved to have been made CEO of the family business"; "Sally may have made her fair share of mistakes in life, but nobody deserves to get cancer."

Even when an innocent or virtuous person meets with a degree of good fortune, something will still feel amiss to us if we judge the "level" of good fortune to fall short of what is deserved. Melvin Lerner concludes from empirical studies in social psychology that "there is no amount of desired resources – money, prestige, power, etc. – that is sufficient to be considered an acceptable fate, if it is less than people believe they deserve" (1981: 21).

I think the only moral concept that might compete on this front with desert is *justice*. When we think that justice has been achieved, then we seemingly are satisfied that no additional redress is needed. But in the end, justice might not actually be a competitor to desert. It might be derivative of it. As Feldman remarks, there is an "ancient and plausible" history of understanding justice as accomplished "when people receive goods and evils according to *desert*" (1995: 573). Louis Pojman adds, "It is interesting to observe how deeply the notion of justice as desert or merit is embedded in human history. It seems a prereflective, basic idea of primordial or Ur-justice. One finds it in every known culture and religion" (1997: 559). Sidgwick weighed in that "when we speak of the world as justly governed by God, we seem to mean that, if we could know the whole of human existence, we should find that happiness is distributed among men according to their desert" (1981: bk. III, ch. v, §5, 280). As for empirical studies, Christopher Freiman and Shaun Nichols report: "Social scientific research repeatedly confirms that lay persons regard desert as *the* principle of distributive justice" (2011: 133).

Given the importance we seem to associate with desert, it is surely worth asking about the particular value we are apparently sensitive to. What exactly is our deep concern when we insist that people should "get what they deserve"? What do we see as so valuable about the conditions for desert being satisfied? And what exactly are those conditions?

4.2 The Value of Proportional Treatment

Keep in mind that ancient philosophers like Plato and Aristotle seemingly viewed justice in terms of desert. Aristotle remarked that "all men think justice to be a sort of equality" (2017: bk. 3, §12, 64). But equality of *what* exactly? Here we have two placeholders to identify: (1) *what* it is that is deserved, and (2) the *basis* on which one is deserving. As for (1), what is deserved is positive or negative *treatment* (or, more broadly, a positive or negative *outcome*, if there is no one to administer the treatment). That is, we treat someone in a way that makes their life go better/worse for them. As for (2), some character trait of a person, perhaps as revealed through some action, is the basis on which the person is deserving.

On Aristotle's model of "equality," the conditions for desert are met when the positive/negative treatment a person receives is equal, or *proportional*, to some trait of the person. Aristotle noted that people of his day disagreed about the relevant trait that would merit positive treatment: "Democrats identify it with the status of freeman, supporters of oligarchy with wealth (or with noble birth), and supporters of aristocracy with excellence" (2016: bk 5, §3, 1131^a, 77). In more recent centuries, most moral philosophers have pointed to moral virtue/viciousness as the key desert basis. When we make value judgments that "this person deserves praise" or "that person deserves prison," we generally have in mind some kind of morally relevant characteristic of the person. (See Kinghorn 2021: ch. 3 for an overview of the debate among moral philosophers on the range of legitimate desert bases.)

So we arrive at the standard account of desert among moral philosophers. Deserved treatment is treatment that positively/negatively affects one's well-being in proportion to one's positive/negative moral character. The important questions still loom: *Why* do we care so much about people getting proportional treatment? What are we perceiving as so valuable about the attainment of this proportionality? I think there are two broad kinds of answers we might give here. And there are profound theological implications stemming from our conclusions about where the value of proportionality lies.

Throughout this discussion, it is important to keep in mind that the value we associate with desert is different than our personal liking and disliking of other people. We don't like the antagonists of Western movies, and so of course we *enjoy* seeing the local sheriff win a gunfight against them. But a concern for desert is again not the same as *schadenfreude*. When witnessing the downfall of someone we loathe, we may remark, "Good, he deserves it!" But as John Kleinig notes, it may be that such desert claims "are not being used to ascribe desert but to express malice" (1973: 87). (David Miller labeled as "sham" desert claims those claims that use the *language* of desert even while they are motiv-ated by personal feeling or by some non-desert, ethical consideration such as entitlement [1999: 133–8].) Similarly, we tend to admire and feel affection toward virtuous people. But we must not confuse the value of positive desert with the delight we naturally feel when people we're fond of meet with good fortune.

Thinking specifically of the value we attach to people getting what they deserve, what do we judge to be so valuable about this outcome? I again think there are two broad theories one might offer. First, it might be that we are simply seeing the intrinsic value in proportionality *itself* obtaining between a person's character and the positive/negative outcomes with which they meet in life. Ross commented,

> Four things, then, seem to be intrinsically good – virtue, pleasure, the alloca-
> tion of pleasure to the virtuous, and knowledge (and in a less degree right
> opinion). And I am unable to discover anything that is intrinsically good,
> which is not either one of these or a combination of two or more of them
> (2002: 140).

Ross's third intrinsic good here of course has to do with desert. There is no further argument on offer for his conclusion that intrinsic value exists in the alignment of pleasurable experiences with virtuous character. Ross insisted that we intuitively "must recognize" it as valuable when pleasures and pains are apportioned, respectively, to virtuous and to vicious people. And in fact we all do have, Ross claimed, a "decided conviction" that it is good for a person to be happy when this happiness is deserved (136, 138).

Ross's view represents much of the received wisdom on desert. Most contemporary philosophers writing on desert affirm that, if a person deserves X, then it follows that there is intrinsic value in the person receiving X. (See Sher 1987: ch. 8 & 11; Miller 1999: 135–6; Pojman 1999: 292; Hurka 2001: 7–8; Kristjánsson 2006: ch. 2; Schmidtz 2006: 85–6; McMahan 2009: 8–9; Kershnar 2010: ch. 1 & 6; Kagan 2012: 17; Berman 2013: 89; Zaibert 2017: 14–16.). Nathan Hannah refers to this view as "the standard view," observing that "many of those who accept it just assume it" (2019: 109–10).

Yet I think there is a second, plausible explanation of why we judge it so valuable that people get what they deserve (see Kinghorn 2021: ch. 4–7). On this alternative account of desert, we perceive proportionality between virtue and happiness as having *instrumental* value. Our ultimate concern is that the *truth* of a person's characteristics be brought to light and acknowledged. What we value so highly is a truthful, shared narrative of who we all are and how we have affected one another. We will feel the need for redress until we are satisfied that the person in question, as well as the community members affected by that person, have jointly acknowledged the truth about that person. The reason we care so much about people "getting what they deserve" is that we have a deep desire to be part of a community of flourishing relationships. And we recognize that a healthy community requires a truthful, shared narrative about who we are as individuals and how we have affected one another.

How do we publicly bring a person's traits and actions to light? Typically, we do so by offering positive/negative treatments of the person (e.g., rewards, tributes, punishments, reprimands) in proportion to her virtuous/vicious character. When the truth about a person's character and impact on a community has been exposed and acknowledged, then we are satisfied that the person has indeed "gotten what she deserved."

In short, there are two ways of interpreting the kind of value to which we are sensitive when we judge that some person *deserves* positive/negative treatment. The more traditional view, articulated by such figures as Kant, Moore, and Ross, is that value exists in the attainment itself of proportionality between positive/negative treatment and a person's virtuous/vicious character. We see this intrinsic value as a matter of clear intuition. An alternative view, however, is that we view proportionality as instrumentally valuable in that it aids in achieving a further end that we find so valuable. This further end is the shared acknowledgment of a person's virtuous/vicious character, as part of a shared, truthful narrative of how we have affected one another in a community. In Section 4.3, I will look at how one might try to adjudicate the two views. I will then turn in Sections 4.4 and 4.5 to some theological implications of these two divergent views on the value of desert.

4.3 The Perceived Value of Truth, Not Proportionality?

The more traditional view of desert does admittedly have a good deal of initial, intuitive force. When we hear of bullies or oppressors or cheats leading the life of Riley, suffering no repercussions for their past actions, it really sticks in our craw. It is not merely that we do not like such people and desire to see their downfall. Rather, as Kristjánsson noted, our feeling is one of moral indignation, a frustration stemming from our "sense of justice." Similarly, we experience a particular kind of frustration when a virtuous person meets with heartache or just bad luck. We may naturally feel sadness when we hear of anyone meeting with tragedy. But if it happens to an especially kind person who has self-sacrificially given to others over the years, we are especially distressed. Shared laments will be offered: "Of all the people for this to happen to, they are the last one who deserves it!"

There is indeed significant, initial plausibility to the view that our concern in making desert claims is for what we might call a *cosmic balance* between people's character traits and the way they are treated. We judge it a good thing, an appropriate thing, when good people meet with good outcomes in life. And frankly we feel that there is a certain appropriateness about bad people meeting with bad outcomes. Perhaps we may have religious or other ethical commitments that *trump* the value of desert in our minds. For instance, the Christian theist may believe that forgiveness or universal charity has greater value than the value of bad people getting what they deserve. Yet, even if we are committed to the ideal of charitable attitudes toward all people, we nevertheless feel that *something* of value is lost when vicious people meet with continuously good fortune. On the traditional view of desert, our desert claims express our concern for a cosmic balance: all people meeting with positive/negative fortune in proportion to their virtuous/vicious character.

Despite the initial plausibility of this interpretation of our concern about desert, I think the alternative view actually fares better on closer analysis. That view again is that our deep concern is that the *truth* about a person's virtue/viciousness be acknowledged – an acknowledgment made possible by, or that even consists in, treatment of the person that is proportional to her moral character.

Here's a methodological point about assessing the two views. There is a core concern that leads us to make claims like "He deserves praise" or "She deserves a reprimand." The interpretive question we are considering is: what kind of value are people sensitive to in making these desert claims? The traditional view of desert is that we are perceiving, or are sensitive to, the intrinsic value of proportionality itself obtaining between character and good/bad fortune. If this is correct, then when we are convinced that proportionality *has* been achieved in some case, our concern should be satisfied that the person has "gotten what they deserved."

But here is where cracks appear in the traditional interpretation of our desert concern. There seem clear cases in which we *are* satisfied that proportionality has been attained, and yet we are *not* satisfied that the person has actually gotten what they deserve. And these kinds of cases lend credence to the alternative interpretation of our concern for desert sketched earlier.

Consider the example of Sacrificial Sue, a social worker who has spent most of her adult life mentoring at-risk youth. Sue's labor goes well beyond her job description. She has worked on weekends without pay, answered emergency phone calls in the middle of the night, and even opened her home to youth who were out of options. Only a few people have any idea of the extent of Sue's ministry. She is one of the unsung heroes of the community.

When Sue retires, what kind of treatment does she deserve? Very positive treatment, for sure. But positive treatment of what kind exactly? Here we reach a key point. Proportionality between positive treatment and virtue can be achieved *in any number of ways*. A variety of treatments can positively impact a person's well-being – for example, rewards, awards, prizes, opportunities, expressions of gratitude or appreciation or approval (see Feinberg 1970).

Positive treatments are thus, as Kristjánsson notes, "substitutable" on the traditional view of desert, which assumes that intrinsic value exists in proportionality itself obtaining between treatment and desert basis (2006: 71).

But against the traditional view, surely we would not be satisfied that Sue has received "what she truly deserved" if just *any* positive treatment were given to her. Suppose that shortly after retirement, Sue wins the lottery. We might judge this positive treatment to actually *exceed* the corresponding, positive "level" of her virtuous character. But I think we would still insist that Sue hasn't received certain kinds of positive treatment she deserved.

When someone retires, it is common to give testimonial dinners or in some other way to acknowledge publicly a person's work contributions and impact on others. Sue deserves to have her work made known – ideally by some of those youth she helped in so many ways. Without the positive treatment of gratitude and praise in response to Sue's actual endeavors, surely our concern will not be satisfied that she has gotten what she truly deserves. A financial gift might be a necessary *part* of her community's genuine acknowledgment of her impact. But the mere, positive outcome of financial good fortune – even winning the lottery – won't by itself satisfy our concern for desert. For this positive treatment won't have brought out the truth about Sue, allowing for a shared acknowledgment of who she is within the community. And so we will still think that Sue deserves something *more* than she has gotten – even as, ironically, we might also conclude that the good fortune of winning a lottery was already more than is proportional to her good character. This shows that proportionality was not actually the deep concern we had when we initially judged that Sue deserved positive treatment.

Similar points apply to cases in which we judge that a vicious person should receive negative treatment. Consider the case of Scamming Sam, who has preyed on a line of low-income families seeking loans. His pattern is to purposely mislead them about the hidden costs of taking out a loan from him. When spiraling interest rates trap the families in ever-increasing payments they are unable to manage, Sam aggressively pursues litigation and secures a percentage of their future income earnings. (The reason Sam targets low-income families is because they are unlikely to have their own legal representation or to contest his maneuvers.) The effects on families are of course devastating. But that's his business plan, and it has made him very wealthy.

A case like this makes our blood boil. We may insist loudly that Scamming Sam is deserving of a particularly bad fate. But what exactly will satisfy our concern for desert in such a case? Just *any* negative outcome? Hurka comments that, "if a vicious person suffers pain unrelated to his vice, that is what common sense calls poetic justice" (2001: 12, ft. 10). Does poetic justice satisfy the ultimate concern behind our desert claims about Sam? Defending the traditional view of desert, Kristjánsson comments that it is perfectly intelligible to talk about "a villain having deservedly been crushed to death in a landslide" (2006: 71). The traditional view again allows for these kinds of substitutable outcomes in satisfying the proportionality condition (purportedly) at the heart of desert.

Against the traditional view of desert, though, I think it's clear that poetic justice *doesn't* itself always satisfy the concern behind our desert claims. Suppose that Sam suffers a long, slow death from cancer. We might estimate that Sam's level of suffering ended up being *more* than his vicious character merited. ("Yes, he was a horrible person, but nobody deserves *that!*") Yet even in such a case, I think we may continue to insist that there is negative treatment that Sam deserved and still has not received. What we think he deserved is some treatment that brought to light his character and actions.

It is instructive to reflect on the criminal trials of individuals like Scamming Sam, who have conned people or abused people or harmed people in some way. At sentencing hearings, victims come forward to testify to the impact that the offender has had on their lives. Even when a mandated prison term is a foregone conclusion, victims still want to be *heard*. They want the offender to *know* how he has affected them: how the financial fraud has caused them various family hardships, how the abuse has led to continued feelings of shame and mistrust of others, and so on. Until the offender has *owned up*, publicly, to the impact he has had on others, we will continue to feel the need for redress. We will continue to feel that the person has not truly gotten what he deserved. (Interestingly, when there *is* this shared acknowledgment, with the offender offering sincere acts of contrition and attempts at restitution, I think our concern that the offender receive proportional, punitive treatment is typically mitigated to a significant degree.)

As one real-life example, at the 2018 trial of Larry Nassar (the former USA gymnastics team doctor), his conviction and sentencing were already foregone conclusions. But many of his victims appeared in court to give statements. They wanted him to know, needed him to know, what exactly he had done to them. It was not enough for them that he broadly acknowledged that he had wronged them. They needed him to know the specific ways he had affected them: the resulting confusion they experienced, the feelings of shame, the fear, the subsequent difficulties trusting others. Plausibly, the deep concern in such cases is for a shared acknowledgment by all parties of the *truth* of how a person has affected others.

These points seem to support the idea that the ultimate concern behind our desert claims is for the public, shared acknowledgment of a truthful narrative of who a person is within a community. Proportional treatment does often bring out that truth. ("Wow, that's a huge fine the EPA administered; that company's environment law violations must have been extensive!") But not always. And when it doesn't, our feeling that further redress is needed seems to point to the conclusion that the value we judge proportionality to have is instrumental – not intrinsic – value.

We have looked at two different interpretations of our judgments that people can be *deserving* of positive or negative treatment. The more traditional view among philosophers is that we perceive (intrinsic) value in proportionality itself obtaining between people's moral character and the positive/negative outcomes they experience. An alternative view is that we are sensitive to the value of a shared, truthful narrative of how people have affected one another – with proportional treatment having instrumental value insofar as it helps bring these facts to light.

4.4 Interpreting God's Concern for Just Outcomes

One's view on the nature of desert judgments will have significant implications for a number of related theological matters. Is God's justice always *restorative* justice? If one's working assumption is that there is no value in proportional treatment for its own sake, then there would be no final value in God punishing individuals. Any negative treatment God bestowed on an individual would only be valuable inasmuch as it helped lead to an outcome that *did* have final value. For instance, God might discipline individuals as a way of prompting repentance, thereby making possible the kind of moral transformation that allows them to take their place within the heavenly community. But in working toward "just" outcomes, God would always be working toward restorative ends.

On the other hand, if one judges there to be value in proportionality itself obtaining between a person's moral character and the treatment she is given, then one will naturally conclude that there is value in God punishing sinners – apart from any restoration that may or may not take place. One may even think that there is value in God *eternally* punishing sinners. Marilyn Adams in recent years contended that no amount of finite, sinful choices in this life could possibly be proportional to an *eternity* of conscious, negative experiences in hell (1975, 1993). But some may still be convinced by Anselm's suggestive reasoning (see his *Cur Deus Homo*) that a sin against an "infinite" God of goodness and authority merits an "infinite" punishment. (See John Lamont 2011 for an overview of philosophers and theologians who have either objected to or sought to defend Anselm's claim.)

Anselm's discussion is in the context of how Christians should understand the Atonement. What exactly was accomplished when Jesus died on the cross and rose again? Anselm's understanding of the Atonement focused on Christ's death "satisfying" God. Anselm seemingly had God's *honor* foremost in mind. Defenders of the "penal substitution" model of the Atonement focus on the way in which God's *justice* is satisfied, as Jesus receives the punitive treatment that is actually proportional to *our* sins (see Craig 2020). If one views the value of desert in terms of proportionality itself obtaining, then one may have reason to embrace this model. For the picture of God that emerges is one who is concerned for the value of retributive justice.

For those who reject this model of desert-based justice, I have suggested that they may view "deserved" treatments as those that make possible a truthful, shared narrative. This shared narrative is a prerequisite for the restoration that God intends for all people. And this restoration is the valuable end associated with God's corrective justice. From this working assumption about the value of desert, one will have reason to embrace a model of the Atonement that does *not* picture God as concerned with retributive justice as an end with final value.

Thus far I have considered how philosophical conclusions about the value of desert may impact theological affirmations. Equally, one may reach a theological conclusion that requires the acceptance of a particular theory of desert. Perhaps one concludes that the biblical passages describing God's *wrath* "poured out against sinful people" really do require us to affirm the value of retributive justice and thus the value of proportionality itself between treatment and moral character. (Though see Kinghorn 2019 for an argument against such a conclusion.) Or perhaps one thinks that the biblical passages about hell require such an affirmation. Or perhaps one's theological tradition emphasizes that the manifestation of God's retributive justice is one way in which God receives *glory.*

Of course, *alternative* theological conclusions about these issues may lead one to embrace the alternative account of desert I have outlined. Perhaps one concludes that the Gospel of John definitively links God's glory with the loving intentions God has for people to flourish. Or perhaps one rejects the claim that God's essential nature (which existed prior to the creation of any world) could include a concern for retributive justice. Or perhaps one is convinced that the biblical passages describing God's justice – even God's wrath – really do have restoration at their heart. One may then think, "Whatever the philosophical arguments for or against the traditional view of desert, I must reject it because it leads to a picture of God (or a model of the atonement, or an interpretation of a key biblical passage) that I have already rejected."

Theologians will continue to debate whether the biblical picture of God's justice is solely restorative or at times also retributive. Each camp will have its own favorite passages to highlight. I will not attempt any extended survey of biblical passages that might be offered to support either of the views I have outlined on the value of desert. Instead, I want to end with a case study of how an analysis of a biblical passage might go. I hope to give an indication of how working assumptions about proportional treatment – specifically, whether there is final value attached to it – can impact how one interprets a given passage.

4.5 A Theological Case Study

The passage I have in mind is Jesus's parable of the rich man and Lazarus, sometimes called Dives and Lazarus.

> [19]There was a rich man who was dressed in purple and fine linen and who feasted sumptuously every day. [20]And at his gate lay a poor man named Lazarus, covered with sores, [21]who longed to satisfy his hunger with what fell from the rich man's table; even the dogs would come and lick his sores. [22]The poor man died and was carried away by the angels to be with Abraham. The rich man also died and was buried. [23]In Hades, where he was being tormented, he looked up and saw Abraham far away with Lazarus by his side. [24]He called out, "Father Abraham, have mercy on me, and send Lazarus to dip the tip of his finger in water and cool my tongue; for I am in agony in these flames." [25]But Abraham said, "Child, remember that during your lifetime you received your good things, and Lazarus in like manner evil things; but now he is comforted here, and you are in agony. [26]Besides all this, between you and us a great chasm has been fixed, so that those who might want to pass from here to you cannot do so, and no one can cross from there to us." [27]He said, "Then, father, I beg you to send him to my father's house – [28]for I have five brothers – that he may warn them, so that they will not also come into this place of torment." [29]Abraham replied, "They have Moses and the prophets; they should listen to them." [30]He said, "No, father Abraham; but if someone goes to them from the dead, they will repent." [31]He said to him, "If they do not listen to Moses and the prophets, neither will they be convinced even if someone rises from the dead." (Luke 16: 19–31)

Two broad interpretations of this passage are possible. The first one naturally flows from a prior acceptance of the traditional view of desert judgments. On this view, there is final value in proportionality itself obtaining between a person's moral character and the treatment they receive. Looking at Jesus's parable, the core point Jesus is trying to make becomes fairly straightforward.

The rich man in the story lived an extravagant earthly life, far better than was proportional to his character. The indication is that his character was quite bad. After all, he knew Lazarus by name. Yet, despite Lazarus languishing right outside his house, he did not offer Lazarus even the scraps off his table – never mind trying to address Lazarus's desperate medical state. As for Lazarus, we are not told much about his character. But if his character was even moderately upright, then his fate on earth was surely significantly worse than was proportional to his character.

In the next life, however, there will be a final reckoning. God will put all things right. And this establishment of justice will involve a great reversal of fortunes for people like the characters in our story. Lazarus, who suffered so disproportionally while on earth, is now taken up to enjoy life in the community that includes Father Abraham. As for the rich man, when he asks Abraham for help in relieving his current suffering, Abraham explains to him that "during your lifetime you received your good things." God's judgment has brought about the current reversal of fortunes. The rich man's treatment is coming into alignment with his true character. A cosmic balance of moral character and outcomes is being established.

There is no indication of any *instrumental* value associated with this balancing of scales, any *further* end which this balancing is achieving. Abraham explains that "a great chasm has been fixed" between the current place of the rich man and the place enjoyed by Abraham and Lazarus. Restoration is not possible. That opportunity has passed. The rich man suggests that his current suffering might yet have instrumental value if it can serve as a warning to his brothers. But Abraham dismisses even that avenue to further, instrumental value. Instead, the clear lesson that emerges from the parable is that there is value in proportionality *itself* being established between people's moral character and the outcomes they experience.

Perhaps Jesus intended to convey multiple messages through this parable. But surely one message is that we should be sensitive to the (final) value of proportionality obtaining between a person's virtue and the treatment she receives.

Well, that's one way to interpret the parable. But what if one's settled judgment is that there is no final value in such proportionality obtaining? Suppose instead that one interprets our concern for desert as a sensitivity to the value of truthful narratives and the healthy, ongoing relationships they make possible. One will then look for alternative interpretations of the parable and of the values to which Jesus may be appealing.

An alternative interpretation begins with the working assumption that, if there is value in the rich man getting negative treatment in line with his negative character, this value must be instrumental. If God is concerned that the rich man "get what he deserves," this concern will end up being a concern for a shared acknowledgment about who the man is and how he has affected others. On this alternative view of the value of desert, a very different interpretation of Jesus's parable starts to take shape. In brief, the parable becomes a description of the rich man's rather audacious attempt at self-justification and his refusal to acknowledge the truth about his past actions toward others.

In the rich man's earthly life, he was heartlessly indifferent to the plight of poor Lazarus. When later he himself is suffering in Hades, he offers no words of

apology to Lazarus. He mentions Lazarus only in the context of telling Abraham
to send Lazarus to help him. The rich man's character clearly needs reforming.
Still, eventual restoration for him has not been ruled out by anything external to
him. The rich man is described as being in Hades (not hell), understood in the
Christian tradition as an intermediate state where one's character can continue
to be shaped. In Abraham's description of the "great chasm" that exists between
himself and the rich man, there is no indication that those on the rich man's side
of the chasm who *want* to cross over cannot do so. Might the rich man want to
cross over?

Well, crossing over would involve repentance, in keeping with all of Jesus's
teachings about the steps toward human redemption. But the rich man's conver-
sation with Abraham is a continued effort at self-justification, which is quite the
opposite of repentance. His words to Abraham are *couched* in the language of
concern for others. He voices his concern that his five brothers avoid the kind of
outcome he is having to endure. ("Then I beg you to send him to my father's
house – for I have five brothers – that he may warn them, so that they will not
also come into this place of torment.") His call here is for his brothers to receive
more information than *he himself* received. The implicit signaling seems clear:
"If *I* had received this information, then I wouldn't have ended up in my current
predicament."

But Abraham's pointed response is that a lack of information is not the
relevant issue. He notes that the rich man's brothers "have Moses and the
prophets." And he declares that "if they do not listen to Moses and the prophets,
neither will they be convinced even if someone rises from the dead." The clear
implication? The *rich man* during his earthly life had Moses and the prophets!
These were messengers from God, with repeated messages about helping the
poor and marginalized. The rich man had not been persuaded by their messages
to give even minimal aid to someone, Lazarus, who was in desperate need. By
implication, neither would the rich man have been persuaded even by
a messenger who rose from the dead.

From this perspective, the parable is not pointing to the final value of the rich
man receiving negative treatment that is in keeping with his previous, negative
character. Rather, the parable is a cautionary tale about a rich man's continued
refusal to cooperate with God's attempts to restore him to a community marked
by self-giving love. The rich man is not offering a lament that it is too late for him,
despite his current desire to be restored to this type of community. Rather, the rich
man is continuing the path of self-justification, refusing to acknowledge the truth
about himself. It may indeed be "too late" for the rich man. But this is not because
God has opted to realize the valued end of meting out proportional treatment.

Rather, it is because the rich man is by now so hardened in self-deception that he would not change his attitudes, even if warned by a person risen from the dead.

I have suggested that one's interpretation of our common value judgments regarding desert may impact one's interpretation of what Jesus is trying to communicate through this parable. Equally, one may find a particular reading of the parable convincing; and that reading may cause one to revise one's previous understanding of the value associated with people getting what they deserve. The potential *problem* here is the familiar one in which one's theological conclusions may be at odds with the value judgments one forms. Of course, there may also be benefits to such tension. One's value judgments may offer new insights into a biblical passage (e.g., about the lessons Jesus wanted us to draw from a parable) or open up new ways of understanding a theological doctrine (like the Atonement).

I think these potential benefits are worth emphasizing as a concluding point. When there is conflict between our value judgments and some particular interpretation of scripture or Christian doctrine, questions of methodology emerge. Our value judgments can be one form of divine communication to us. *Should* our value judgments be equal to, or even trump, other sources of theology? Theists may offer a range of answers to this question of theological method. But what is clear is that humans do continually make value judgments – notably about what a good life is and about who deserves a good life. A religious instructor might see our value judgments as a problem if they conflict in some instance with a favored theological position. A religious instructor might also see them as an indispensable part of human psychology in need of nurturing and development. This latter approach seems to me much the wiser one.

References

Adams, M. M. (1975). Hell and the God of justice. *Religious Studies*, 11(4), 433–47.

Adams, M. M. (1993). The problem of hell: A problem of evil for Christians. In E. Stump and N. Kretzmann, eds., *Reasoned Faith: Essays in Philosophical Theology in Honor of Norman Kretzmann*, Ithaca, NY: Cornell University Press, pp. 301–27.

Adams, R. M. (1999). *Finite and Infinite Goods*, New York: Oxford University Press.

Alfano, M. (2012). Expanding the situationist challenge to responsibilist virtue epistemology. *Philosophical Quarterly*, 62(247), 223–49.

Alfano, M., Machery, E., Plakias, A., and Loeb, D. (2018). Experimental moral philosophy. *The Stanford Encyclopedia of Philosophy*, E. Zalta, ed., plato .stanford.edu/archives/win2018/entries/experimental-moral.

Anderson, S. W., Bechara, A., Damasio, H., Tranel, D., and Damasio, A. R. (1999). Impairment of social and moral behavior related to early damage in human prefrontal cortex. *Nature Neuroscience*, 2(11), 1032–7.

Aquinas, T. (1947). *Summa Theologica*, Fathers of the English Dominican Province, trans., New York: Benziger Brothers.

Aristotle (2016). *Nicomachean Ethics*, W. D. Ross, trans., Digireads.com.

Aristotle (2017). *Politics*, B. Jowett, trans., Digireads.com.

Augustine (1887). *On the Trinity*, A. Haddan, trans. In P. Schaff, ed., *Nicene and Post-Nicene Fathers*, vol. 3, Buffalo, NY: Christian Literature.

Augustine (2009). *On Christian Doctrine*, J. Shaw, ed., Mineola, NY: Dover.

Augustine (2015). *Confessions*, E. B. Pusey, trans., Digireads.com.

Baggett, D., and Walls, J. (2011). *Good God*, New York: Oxford University Press.

Barth, K. (1938). *The Knowledge of God and the Service of God according to Teaching of the Reformation (Gifford Lectures)*, J. Haire and I. Henderson, trans., London: Hodder and Stoughton.

Barth, K. (2004). *Church Dogmatics, vol. I, pt. I: The Doctrine of the Word of God*, G. Bromiley, trans., G. Bromiley and T. Torrance, eds., London: T & T Clark.

Bechara, A. (2004). The role of emotion in decision-making: Evidence from neurological patients with orbitofrontal damage. *Brain and Cognition*, 55(1), 30–40.

Berman, M. (2013). Rehabilitating retributivism. *Law and Philosophy*, 32(1), 83–108.

Budziszewki, J. (2011). *What We Can't Know: A Guide*, rev. ed., San Francisco: Ignatius Press.

Butler, J. (2017). *Fifteen Sermons and Other Writings on Ethics*, D. McNaughton, ed., Oxford: Oxford University Press.

Chapman, H., and Anderson, A. (2013). Things rank and gross in nature: A review and synthesis of moral disgust. *Psychological Bulletin*, 139(2), 300–27.

Cottingham, J. (2011). The source of goodness. In H. Harris, ed., *God, Goodness, and Philosophy*, New York: Routledge, pp. 49–62.

Craig, W. L. (2020). *Atonement and the Death of Christ*, Waco, TX: Baylor University Press.

Cushman, F. (2013). Action, outcome, and value: A dual-system framework for morality. *Personality and Social Psychology Review*, 17(3), 273–92.

Dancy, J. (1993). *Moral Reasons*, Oxford: Blackwell.

Darwall, S. (2002). *Welfare and Rational Care*, Princeton, NJ: Princeton University Press.

Doris, J. (2002). *Lack of Character: Personality and Moral Behavior*, Cambridge: Cambridge University Press.

Edwards, J. (1835). The eternity of hell torments. In H. Rogers, ed., *The Works of Jonathan Edwards*, vol. 1, New York: Daniel Appleton & Company, pp. 83–9.

Erasmus, D. (1969). On the freedom of the will. In E. Rupp and A. Marlow, eds., *Luther and Erasmus: Free Will and Salvation*, E. Rupp, trans., Philadelphia, PA: Westminster Press.

Evans, J. (2012). Questions and challenges for the new psychology of reasoning. *Thinking and Reasoning*, 18(1), 5–31.

Feinberg, J. (1970). Justice and personal desert. In *Doing and Deserving*, Princeton, NJ: Princeton University Press.

Feldman, F. (1995). Adjusting utility for justice: A consequentialist reply to the objection from justice. *Philosophy and Phenomenological Research*, 55(3), 567–85.

Finlay, S. (2014). *Confusion of Tongues: A Theory of Normative Language*, New York: Oxford University Press.

Freiman, C., and Nichols, S. (2011). Is desert in the details? *Philosophy and Phenomenological Research*, 82(1), 121–33.

Geach, P. (1956). Good and evil. *Analysis*, 17(2), 33–42.

Gill, M., and Nichols, S. (2008). Sentimentalist pluralism: Moral psychology and philosophical ethics. *Philosophical Issues*, 18(1), 143–63.

Goldie, P. (2000). *The Emotions: A Philosophical Exploration*, Oxford: Clarendon.

Green, J., ed. (2011). *Dictionary of Scripture and Ethics*, Grand Rapids, MI: Baker Academic.

Greene, J., and Haidt, J. (2002). How (and where) does moral judgment work? *Trends in Cognitive Sciences*, 6(12), 517–23.

Greene, J., Sommerville, R., Nystrom, L., Darley, J., and Cohen, J. (2001). An fMRI investigation of emotional engagement in moral judgment. *Science*, 293(5537), 2105–8.

Griffin, J. (1996). *Value Judgment: Improving Our Ethical Beliefs*, Oxford: Clarendon.

Haidt, J. (2001). The emotional dog and its rational tail: A social intuitionist approach to moral judgment. *Psychological Review*, 108(4), 814–34.

Haidt, J. (2012). *The Righteous Mind*, New York: Pantheon.

Hannah, N. (2019). Hitting retributivism where it hurts. *Criminal Law and Philosophy*, 3(1), 109–27.

Hill, D. (2005). *Divinity and Maximal Greatness*, New York: Routledge.

Horgan, T., and Tienson, J. (2002). The intentionality of phenomenology and the phenomenology of intentionality. In D. Chalmers, ed., *Philosophy of Mind: Classical and Contemporary Readings*, New York: Oxford University Press, pp. 520–33.

Huemer, M. (2005). *Ethical Intuitionism*, New York: Palgrave Macmillan.

Humberstone, L. (1992). Direction of fit. *Mind*, 101(401), 59–83.

Hurka, T. (2001). The common structure of virtue and desert. *Ethics*, 112(1), 6–31.

James, W. (1884). What is an emotion? *Mind*, 9, 188–205.

Kagan, S. (2012). *The Geometry of Desert*, New York: Oxford University Press.

Kahane, G. (2012). On the wrong track: Process and content in moral psychology. *Mind & Language*, 27(5), 519–45.

Kahneman, D. (2011). *Thinking Fast and Slow*, New York: Macmillan.

Kant, I. (1899). *Critique of Pure Reason*, J. M. D. Meiklejohn, trans., New York: Colonial Press.

Kauppinen, A. (2013). A Humean theory of moral intuition. *Canadian Journal of Philosophy*, 43(3),360–81.

Kauppinen, A. (2015). Intuition and belief in moral motivation. In G. Björnsson, C. Strandberg, R. F. Olinder, J. Eriksson, and F. Björklund, eds., *Moral Internalism*, New York: Oxford University Press, pp. 237–59.

Kauppinen, A. (2018). Moral sentimentalism. *The Stanford Encyclopedia of Philosophy*, E. Zalta, ed., plato.stanford.edu/archives/win2018/entries/moral-sentimentalism.

Kenny, A. (1963). *Action, Emotion and Will*, New York: Routledge and Kegan Paul.

Kershnar, S. (2010). *Desert and Virtue: A Theory of Intrinsic Value*, Lanham, MD: Lexington Books.

Kinghorn, K. (2005). *The Decision of Faith*, London: T & T Clark.

Kinghorn, K. (2016). *A Framework for the Good*, Notre Dame, IN: University of Notre Dame Press.

Kinghorn, K. (2019). *But What about God's Wrath?* Downers Grove, IL: InterVarsity Press.

Kinghorn, K. (2021). *The Nature of Desert Claims*, Cambridge: Cambridge University Press.

Kleinig, J. (1973). *Punishment and Desert*, The Hague: Martinus Nijhoff.

Koenigs, M., Young, L., Adolphs, R., et al. (2007). Damage to the prefrontal cortex increases utilitarian moral judgments. *Nature*, 446(7138), 908–11.

Korsgaard, C. (1983). Two distinctions in goodness. *Philosophical Review*, 92(2), 169–95.

Kriegel, U. (2013). The phenomenal intentionality research program. In U. Kriegel, ed., *Phenomenal Intentionality*, New York: Oxford University Press.

Kriegel, U. (2015). *The Varieties of Consciousness*, New York: Oxford University Press.

Kristjánsson, K. (2006). *Justice and Desert-Based Emotions*, Aldershot: Ashgate.

Lamont, J. (2011). The justice and goodness of hell. *Faith and Philosophy*, 28(2), 152–73.

Lange, C. (1885/1912). The mechanism of the emotions. In B. Rand, trans., *The Classical Psychologists*. Boston, MA: Houghton Mifflin, pp. 672–84.

Lerner, M. (1981). The justice motive in human relations: Some thoughts on what we know and need to know about justice. In M. Lerner and S. Lerner, eds., *The Justice Motive in Social Behavior: Adapting to Times of Scarcity and Change*, New York: Plenum Press, pp. 11–35.

Locke, J. (1975). *An Essay Concerning Human Understanding*, P. Nidditch, ed., Oxford: Clarendon.

Luther, M. (2012). *The Bondage of the Will*, J. Packer and O Johnston, trans., Grand Rapids, MI: Baker Academic.

MacIntyre, A. (1998). *A Short History of Ethics*, London: Routledge.

McDowell, J. (1979). Virtue and reason. *The Monist*, 62(3), 331–50.

McMahan, J. (2009). *Killing in War*, Oxford: Clarendon.

McNaughton, D. (1988). *Moral Vision*, Oxford: Blackwell.

Miller, D. (1999). *Principles of Social Justice*, Cambridge, MA: Harvard University Press.

Moore, G. E. (1993). *Principia Ethica*, rev. ed., Cambridge: Cambridge University Press.

Nagasawa, Y. (2017). *Maximal God: A New Defence of Perfect Being Theism*, Oxford: Oxford University Press.

Nagel, T. (1970). *The Possibility of Altruism*, Princeton, NJ: Princeton University Press.

Nagel, T. (1974). What is it like to be a bat? *Philosophical Review*, 83(4), 435–50.

O'Donovan, O. (2021). "Good, goods, and doing good." Lecture at the Henry Centre, April 15, 2021, https://henrycenter.tiu.edu/videos/#video-26695.

Piller, C. (2014). What is goodness good for? In M. Timmons, ed., *Oxford Studies in Normative Ethics: Vol. 4*, Oxford: Oxford University Press, pp. 179–209.

Plantinga, A. (2000). *Warranted Christian Belief*, New York: Oxford University Press.

Platts, M. (1979). *Ways of Meaning*, London: Routledge and Kegan Paul.

Pojman, L. (1997). Equality and desert. *Philosophy*, 72(282), 549–70.

Pojman, L. (1999). Does equality trump desert? In L. Pojman and O. McLeod, eds., *What Do We Deserve?* Oxford: Oxford University Press.

Prinz, J. (2007). *The Emotional Construction of Morals*, Oxford: Oxford University Press.

Railton, P. (2014). The affective dog and its rational tale: Intuition and attunement. *Ethics*, 124(4), 813–59.

Raz, J. (1999). *Engaging Reason: On the Theory of Value and Action*, Oxford: Oxford University Press.

Richards, L. (1995). *Expository Dictionary of Bible Words*, Grand Rapids, MI: Zondervan.

Roberts, R. C. (2003). *Emotions: An Essay in Aid of Moral Psychology*, Cambridge: Cambridge University Press.

Ross, W. D. (2002). *The Good and the Right*, Oxford: Clarendon.

Scanlon, T. (1998). *What We Owe to Each Other*, Cambridge, MA: Belknap Press.

Scarantino, A., and de Sousa, R. (2021). Emotion. *The Stanford Encyclopedia of Philosophy*, E. Zalta, ed., plato.stanford.edu/archives/sum2021/entries/emotion.

Schmidtz, D. (2006). *The Elements of Justice*, Cambridge: Cambridge University Press.

Schnall, S., Haidt, J., Clore, G., and Jordan, A. (2008). Disgust as embodied moral judgment. *Personality and Social Psychology Bulletin*, 34(8), 1096–1109.

Schroeder, M. (2008). What is the Frege–Geach problem? *Philosophy Compass*, 3(4), 703–20.

Shafer-Landau, R. (2003). *Moral Realism: A Defence*, Oxford: Clarendon.

Sher, G. (1987). *Desert*, Princeton, NJ: Princeton University Press.

Sidgwick, H. (1981). *The Methods of Ethics*, 7th ed., Indianapolis, IN: Hackett.

Sinhababu, N. (2017). *Humean Nature*, Oxford: Oxford University Press.

Stocker, M. (1979). Desiring the bad: An essay in moral psychology. *Journal of Philosophy*, 76(12), 738–53.

Sumner, L. W. (1996). *Welfare, Happiness, and Ethics*, Oxford: Clarendon.

Swinburne, R. (2007). *Revelation: From Metaphor to Analogy*, 2nd ed., Oxford: Clarendon.

Swinburne, R. (2016). *The Coherence of Theism*, 2nd ed., Oxford: Clarendon.

Tappolet, C. (2018). Précis of emotions, values, and agency. *Philosophy and Phenomenological Research*, 97(2), 494–9.

Thagard, P., and Finn, T. (2011). Conscience: What is a moral intuition? In C. Bagnoli, ed., *Moral Motivation and the Emotions*, New York: Oxford University Press, pp. 150–69.

Thomson, J. (2008). *Normativity*, Chicago, IL: Open Court.

Valdesolo, P., and DeSteno, D. (2006). Manipulations of emotional context shape moral judgment. *Psychological Science*, 17(6): 476–7.

Vargas, M. (2013). Situationism and moral responsibility: Free will in fragments. In T. Vierkant, J. Kiverstein and A. Clark, eds.,*Decomposing the Will*, New York: Oxford University Press.

Walls, J., and Baggett, D. (2011). *Good God*, New York: Oxford University Press.

Walton, J. (2009). *The Lost World of Genesis One*, Downers Grove, IL: InterVarsity Press.

Wedgwood, R. (2007). *The Nature of Normativity*, Oxford: Clarendon.

Weinandy, T. (2000). *Does God Suffer?* Notre Dame, IN: University of Notre Dame Press.

Wesley, J. (2022). Sermon 106 on faith. In T. Jackson, ed., *The Works of John Wesley*, WordsOfWesley.com.

Williams, B. (1985). *Ethics and the Limits of Philosophy*, Cambridge, MA: Harvard University Press.

Williamson, T. (2000). *Knowledge and Its Limits*, Oxford: Oxford University Press.

Wolterstorff, N. (1995). *Divine Discourse*, Cambridge: Cambridge University Press.

Young, L., and Koenigs, M. (2007). Investigation emotion in moral cognition: A review of evidence from functional neuroimaging and neuropsychology. *British Medical Bulletin*, 84(1), 69–79.

Zagzebski, L. (2003). Emotion and moral judgment. *Philosophy and Phenomenological Research*, 66(1), 104–24.

Zaibert, L. (2017). On the matter of suffering: Derek Parfit and the possibility of deserved punishment. *Criminal Law and Philosophy*, 11(1), 1–18.

Ziff, P. (1960). *Semantic Analysis*, Ithaca, NY: Cornell University Press.

Cambridge Elements $\equiv$

The Problems of God

Series Editor
Michael L. Peterson
Asbury Theological Seminary

Michael L. Peterson is Professor of Philosophy at Asbury Theological Seminary. He is the author of *God and Evil* (Routledge); *Monotheism, Suffering, and Evil* (Cambridge University Press); *With All Your Mind* (University of Notre Dame Press); *C. S. Lewis and the Christian Worldview* (Oxford University Press); *Evil and the Christian God* (Baker Book House); and *Philosophy of Education: Issues and Options* (Intervarsity Press). He is co-author of *Reason and Religious Belief* (Oxford University Press); *Science, Evolution, and Religion: A Debate about Atheism and Theism* (Oxford University Press); and *Biology, Religion, and Philosophy* (Cambridge University Press). He is editor of *The Problem of Evil: Selected Readings* (University of Notre Dame Press). He is co-editor of *Philosophy of Religion: Selected Readings* (Oxford University Press) and *Contemporary Debates in Philosophy of Religion* (Wiley-Blackwell). He served as General Editor of the Blackwell monograph series Exploring Philosophy of Religion and is founding Managing Editor of the journal *Faith and Philosophy*.

About the Series
This series explores problems related to God, such as the human quest for God or gods, contemplation of God, and critique and rejection of God. Concise, authoritative volumes in this series will reflect the methods of a variety of disciplines, including philosophy of religion, theology, religious studies, and sociology.

Cambridge Elements ☰

The Problems of God

Elements in the Series

A full series listing is available at: www.cambridge.org/EPOG

Printed in the United States
by Baker & Taylor Publisher Services